Strategic Thinking
and Planning

Strategic Thinking and Planning

Second Edition

DARYL FISCHER AND LAURA B. ROBERTS

ROWMAN & LITTLEFIELD
Lanham • Boulder • New York • London

Published by Rowman & Littlefield
A wholly owned subsidiary of The Rowman & Littlefield Publishing Group, Inc.
4501 Forbes Boulevard, Suite 200, Lanham, Maryland 20706
www.rowman.com

Unit A, Whitacre Mews, 26-34 Stannary Street, London SE11 4AB

British Library Cataloguing in Publication Information Available

Library of Congress Cataloging-in-Publication Data Available

ISBN 9781538108451 (pbk. : alk. paper)
ISBN 9781538108383 (electronic)

♾™ The paper used in this publication meets the minimum requirements of
American National Standard for Information Sciences—Permanence of Paper
for Printed Library Materials, ANSI/NISO Z39.48-1992.

Printed in the United States of America

Contents

Foreword

Thank you for your purchase of *Strategic Thinking and Planning*. Since its founding, the Museum Trustee Association (MTA) has communicated strategies and best practices to museums across the Americas. We are especially proud of this new edition of our *Templates for Trustees* series, which digs deeper into trusteeship than ever before and provides the tools for an institution of any size to build, educate, and inspire a successful board.

Throughout the following pages are guidelines and best practices from industry leaders, both staff and volunteers. You will also find eighteen customizable and automated templates to help you keep your board organized and focused on the key issues and challenges facing your museum today. MTA staff is available to you for support as you work your way through the software.

MTA is the network for informing, advising, and inspiring museum trustees. For more information on our products, publications, and services, visit us at www.museumtrustee.org or call our offices. We look forward to hearing from you!

Leland W. Peterson
Board Chairman
Museum Trustee Association

Mary Baily Wieler
President
Museum Trustee Association

About *Templates for Trustees*

"When it comes to board information," says Harvard University professor Richard Chait, "less is more, and much less is much more."[1] Trustees usually receive too much information with too little meaning. Instead, they need structured, concise materials that enhance board performance and satisfaction. This is especially true when it comes to measuring progress on achieving strategic initiatives. Technology can direct trustees' attention to what matters most, helping them gather relevant information and explore it from different perspectives. The templates in this volume, such as operating plan and budget worksheets and dashboard reports, offer streamlined and strategic formats for reporting to the board.

Templates for Trustees is a four-part series designed by the Museum Trustee Association (MTA) to focus attention on the processes and tasks of governance. It supports the MTA's mission "to enhance the effectiveness of museum trustees" by

- promoting and facilitating dialogue between museum trustees and museum directors
- collecting and disseminating information on museum governance that will assist trustees in discharging their responsibilities more effectively
- providing education and training opportunities for museum trustees
- initiating and conducting research on issues of concern to museum trustees

The templates are tools that present board information so that it can be collected, explored, and understood from different perspectives. Each one helps boards create documents, spreadsheets, and presentations tailored to their own needs. Using fill-in-the-blank forms, surveys, and rating scales that are provided on a unique cloud-based app, trustees or administrators enter specific information about their museum and their board. The completed templates and reports serve as starting points to help boards organize their thoughts, identify their priorities, and plan their actions.

Strategic Thinking and Planning is the fourth publication in the four-part series. The other volumes include *Building Museum Boards* (volume 1), *The Leadership Partnership* (volume 2), and *Executive Transitions* (volume 3). All books in the series are available on a web-based application that is accessible to both PC and Mac users.

All four volumes include five sections:

- **Using the *Templates for Trustees* Online App** provides an overview of how the website is structured and a brief description of the purpose and functionality of each template and report. Specific instructions for working with the document library and web-based forms and customizing the templates for each museum's needs are available on the website. This online **Help Manual** will be useful to the administrator, the staff or board member who will modify the forms so they are tailored to individual boards.

- The **User's Guide** distinguishes how strategic thinking and planning differs from other, more familiar strategic planning processes. It will provide a helpful background for all members of the Strategic Planning Team.
- The introduction, **A New Approach to a Familiar Exercise**, summarizes relevant issues and trends and sets the stage for this work.
- **Chapters 1–7** lay out the planning process and present examples of the templates.
- The **Resource Guide** includes publications, websites, and organizations with additional information on strategic planning.

TERMINOLOGY

In these volumes we have used the following terms:

- *Template* refers to any tool that is modified by the administrator and filled out by Strategic Planning Team members.
- *Template library* includes the complete set of tools: surveys, database forms, documents, calendars, and presentations.
- *Reports* are generated by compiling the responses to completed templates.
- *Trustee* refers to a member of the museum's governing board. The terms *board member* and *trustee* are used interchangeably throughout this manual.
- *Director* is the staff leader who reports to the board. Some museums may use *executive director*, *chief executive officer (CEO)*, or *president*.
- *Board chair* is the senior board member who oversees all board functions. Some boards may use *chief volunteer officer (CVO)* or *president*.
- *Executive Committee* refers to the board chair and other officers.
- *Administrator* is the individual—typically a staff member in the executive office—who modifies and manages the templates and serves as liaison between Strategic Planning Team members, the board, and the staff.
- *Strategic Planning Team* is the group charged with creating the strategic plan by engaging in a rigorous process of strategic thinking. It should include a carefully chosen group of board, staff, and community members.
- *Strategic Planning Team Chair* is the individual—typically a member of the board—who leads the Strategic Planning Team and serves as a liaison with the museum's internal and external stakeholders.
- *Facilitator* is the individual or firm charged with guiding the various steps of the planning process and facilitating the meetings, in collaboration with the Strategic Planning Team chair. Whether paid or volunteer, this position is crucial to the success of the entire process.
- *Strategic initiatives* are broad but coherent approaches to achieve the museum's mission and vision with available resources. They suggest a general direction rather than a specific course of action.
- *Goals* are outcome statements that tell how the museum will address, resolve, or accomplish a strategic initiative. In short, they articulate what will be accomplished. More fluid than strategic initiatives, goals can be adjusted and adapted with changing circumstances.
- *Objectives* are precise, measurable, time-phased results that support the achievement of goals. They spell out how goals will be accomplished, by whom, and often for whose benefit.

TEMPLATE SUPPORT

The Museum Trustee Association provides support to boards that purchase *Templates for Trustees*. Please contact the MTA at Support@MuseumTrusteeTemplates.org

- for more information or to order additional volumes in the series
- with questions about tailoring or troubleshooting your templates (service included in the one-time setup fee)
- if you would like to make a testimonial about your experience using this or other volumes in the *Templates for Trustees* series.

NOTE

1. Chait made this observation during a panel on "The New Work of the Nonprofit Board" at the American Association of Museums Annual Meeting in Baltimore, Maryland, in April 2000.

Using the *Templates for Trustees* Online App

The physical book you are holding in your hands is just one part of *Strategic Thinking and Planning*. The templates themselves, which can be tailored to your institution, are stored in an online application hosted by the Museum Trustee Association (MTA). To activate your account in the application, you will need to contact the MTA at support@museumtrusteetemplates.org, pay a modest one-time setup fee (waived for MTA members), and schedule a time to set up your account. Once you create an account, you can begin to review and customize the eighteen templates in *Strategic Thinking and Planning*.

Throughout *Strategic Thinking and Planning* and the other books in the series, there is an important role for the "administrator" who manages the museum's use of the online application. In a larger museum, there may be someone who already manages board communication as part of his or her job. In a smaller museum, the administrator may be the director or a board member. It is also possible for two people to share this role. Once the individual who will fill that role has been identified, he or she should set up the application.

INITIAL SETUP

Step one is registering your account with the Museum Trustee Association by sending an email to support@ museumtrusteetemplates.org. The MTA staff member responsible for administering *Templates for Trustees* will send the administrator a short version of your museum's name (Museum ID), the administrator's username, and a password, which will ensure the privacy and security of your museum's information. MTA staff will also schedule a telephone call to go through the rest of the setup process.

Step two is logging into the application at www.museumtrusteetemplates.org. The first screen (figure 0.1) is the *Templates for Trustees* landing page, with general information about the MTA. From there, click "Log in" on the blue bar to continue. Enter the information provided by MTA (figure 0.2). After logging in, you will be on the landing page for the four volumes in *Templates for Trustees* (figure 0.3).

Step three: Before setting up any single volume, the administrator should establish the global settings. This will enable the application to customize the templates (figure 0.4). Click on "Settings" to launch the page with the placeholder settings. For each item in Settings—the museum name, mission statement, director's name, the title used by the director, and the first month of the museum's fiscal year, annual meeting, or the start of the board cycle—click on "Edit" and put the appropriate information in the field labeled "Setting Value." Click "Save," and you will be returned to the list of Settings. *Note*: You will not see the changes immediately. Close this menu and reopen "Settings" to see the changes.

For the Settings menu and most of the screenshots that follow, the information is for a fictitious museum—the Greenville Museum of Art and History—and its board.

FIGURE 0.1
MTA *Templates for Trustees* Home Page (Courtesy of the Museum Trustee Association)

FIGURE 0.2
MTA *Templates for Trustees* Log In (Courtesy of the Museum Trustee Association)

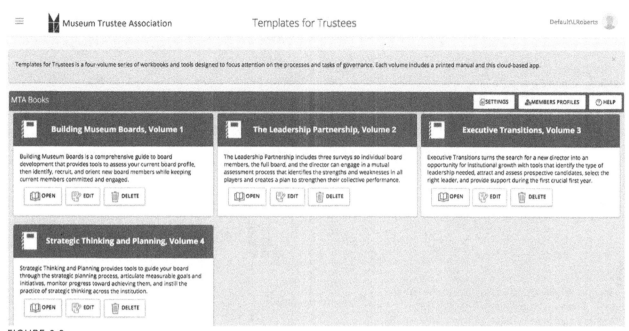

FIGURE 0.3

MTA *Templates for Trustees* Four Volumes Landing Page (Courtesy of the Museum Trustee Association)

Step four is creating a *Templates for Trustees* user account for everyone currently on the board, the director, and the administrator. Next to the MTA logo is a three-bar icon that opens the "Administration" menu (figure 0.5). Click that, and a new column will open on the left side with an arrow next to "Administration" (figure 0.6). Click on the arrow to open the menu and select "Users" (figure 0.7).

Click on the blue "Create New User" box (figure 0.8).

A window will pop up (figure 0.9) where you can enter basic information for each member of the board: name, email address, and a username. We suggest deciding on a convention for creating usernames: *first initial last name* is common. Note that the system will automatically send the new user an email with instructions for choosing a personal password.

Settings/Placeholders

ADD

Description	Value		
The title used by the director	Executive Director	EDIT	DELETE
The director's name	Jordan Charles	EDIT	DELETE
The museum's mission statement	Greenville Museum of Art and History broadens and deepens the community's connections to the heritage and culture of the region.	EDIT	DELETE
Month of the annual meeting and board elections	January	EDIT	DELETE
The name of the museum	Greenville Museum of Art and History	EDIT	DELETE

CLOSE

FIGURE 0.4

MTA *Templates for Trustees* Global Settings (Courtesy of the Museum Trustee Association)

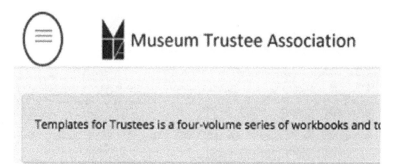

FIGURE 0.5
Strategic Thinking and Planning Administration
Menu Opener (Courtesy of the Museum Trustee
Association)

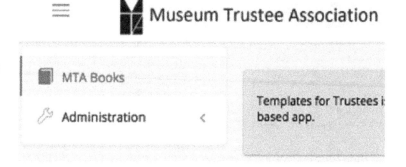

FIGURE 0.6
Strategic Thinking and Planning Administration
Menu Selections (Courtesy of the Museum
Trustee Association)

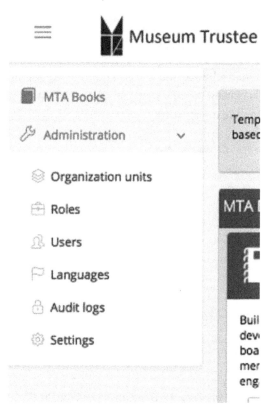

FIGURE 0.7
Strategic Thinking and Planning Administration Menu Selector
(Courtesy of the Museum Trustee Association)

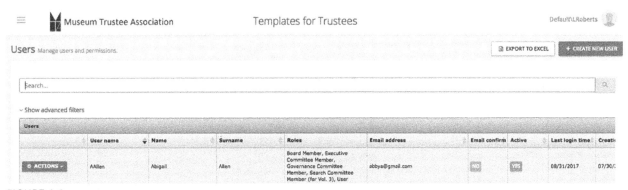

FIGURE 0.8
Strategic Thinking and Planning New User Setup (Courtesy of the Museum Trustee Association)

Every user has one or more "roles" that determine their access to various features. In general, the roles are members and chair of the relevant committee (for this template, the Strategic Planning Team), board members, Executive Committee members, board chair, executive director, community member, volunteer, and administrator. Just above the user's name, you will see "Roles" and a number in a blue circle. At first, that number will be "1" for the basic role of User. To add roles, click that circle. A menu of further roles opens; check all roles that user has and save (figure 0.10).

Create new user   ×

User informations   Roles ❶

                    Name
                    ─────────────────────────

                    Surname

Email address
─────────────────────────────────

Phone number
─────────────────────────────────

User name
─────────────────────────────────

✓ Set random password.
✓ Should change password on next login.
✓ Send activation email.
✓ Active
✓ Is lockout enabled ?

FIGURE 0.9
Strategic Thinking and Planning New User Activation (Courtesy of the Museum Trustee Association)

CANCEL   💾 SAVE

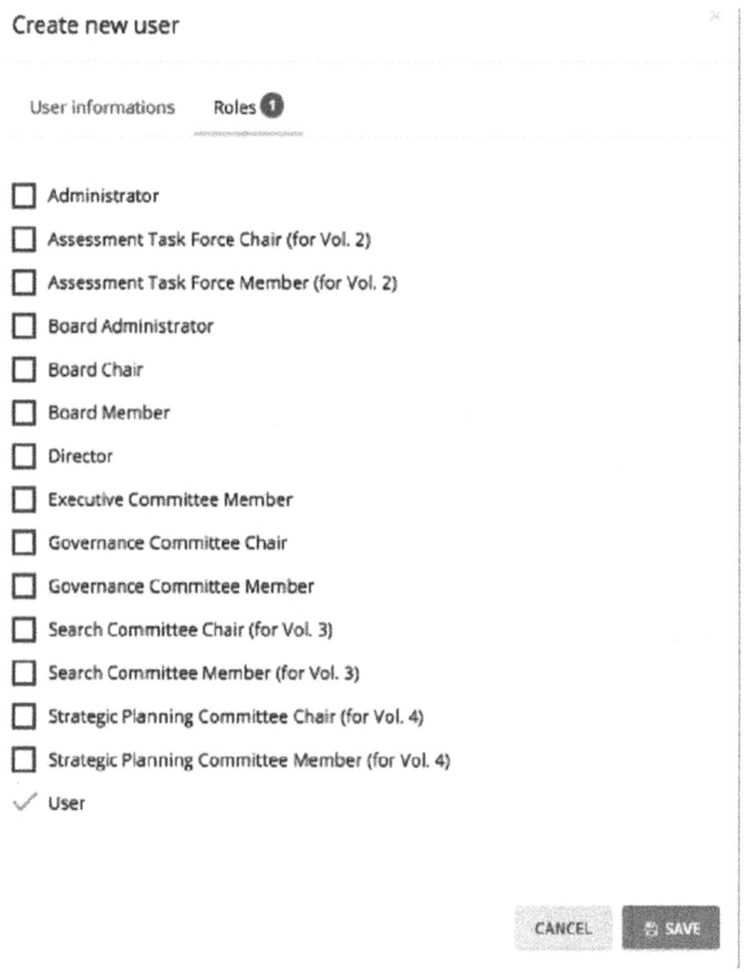

Create new user   ×

User informations   Roles ❶

☐ Administrator

☐ Assessment Task Force Chair (for Vol. 2)

☐ Assessment Task Force Member (for Vol. 2)

☐ Board Administrator

☐ Board Chair

☐ Board Member

☐ Director

☐ Executive Committee Member

☐ Governance Committee Chair

☐ Governance Committee Member

☐ Search Committee Chair (for Vol. 3)

☐ Search Committee Member (for Vol. 3)

☐ Strategic Planning Committee Chair (for Vol. 4)

☐ Strategic Planning Committee Member (for Vol. 4)

✓ User

                                                    CANCEL   ⟳ SAVE

FIGURE 0.10
Strategic Thinking and Planning User Roles
(Courtesy of the Museum Trustee Association)

Because each of the roles will have different needs for information, there are different levels of access to templates and reports. Aside from the administrator, the chair of the Strategic Planning Team will have the most extensive access to the files in this volume. Members of the Strategic Planning Team will have greater access than other members of the board so that they can do the work of the task force. (Please note: Because this list of users is accessed by all of the *Templates for Trustees*, there are roles that are not relevant to *Strategic Thinking and Planning*. The administrator can add those roles when setting up other volumes.)

All of the users are entered into a table for further customizing and editing (figure 0.11). Click the blue "Actions" button next to the user's name and select "Edit." There is also a button that allows the administrator to "Create New User," which brings up the same screen shown in figure 0.9.

Every user must have an email address associated with their user profile. If one or more board members do not use email, we suggest setting up an account on the museum's email system, with mail forwarded to the administrator. That way, whenever an email is generated for the board member(s), the administrator will receive the intended survey, report, form, or document and can print a hard copy to send to the board member(s) by mail or arrange for it to be picked up at the museum.

Step five: Having set up all of the museum's users, it is time to start using the templates. Return to the three-bar menu next to the MTA logo and select "MTA Books" (figure 0.12), which will bring you back to the landing

FIGURE 0.11
Strategic Thinking and Planning User Edits (Courtesy of the Museum Trustee Association)

FIGURE 0.12
MTA *Templates for Trustees* Four Volumes Landing Page (Courtesy of the Museum Trustee Association)

page for the four volumes in *Templates for Trustees*. Because you have purchased *Strategic Thinking and Planning*, those templates will be live.

In addition to these basic instructions, *Templates for Trustees* has an online Help function with more detailed and specific instructions. The "Help" button is always on the blue bar, next to "Members Profiles" (figure 0.13).

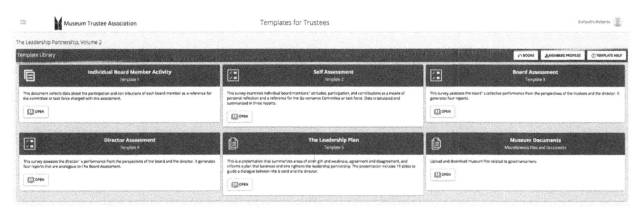

FIGURE 0.13
Templates for Trustees Help Button (Courtesy of the Museum Trustee Association)

Strategic Thinking and Planning
User's Guide

Setting the course that their institutions will follow into the future is among the highest priorities of museum leaders, whether they are paid staff members or volunteer board members. Though no one would deny the importance of paying attention to the day-to-day issues that affect visitors and staff, articulating the museum's mission and vision and developing robust plans to achieve those ambitions are among the greatest contributions that directors and trustees make during their tenure. Once they have established those institutional touchstones, their ultimate responsibility is to monitor progress continually and regularly toward realizing strategic goals in the interests of the communities served by the museum.

This book and the accompanying templates will model the kind of thinking that is required not only to create a strategic plan that is tailored to each institution but also to stay focused on the strategic aspects of governance while implementing that plan. In reading the pages that follow, planning teams will be introduced to exercises and tools that will help them focus on what's most important to the future of their institution. In using the templates, they will adopt new ways of analyzing information and thinking about their museum's mission that will make them more effective leaders.

The process and the resulting strategic plan will coalesce the energies of trustees, staff members, volunteers, and community partners around strategic priorities-building efficiencies and increasing synergies. It will

- establish a common ground, with everyone working toward shared goals and outcomes
- build better communication between and among internal and external stakeholders
- build teamwork across museum departments and among board and staff members
- broaden and strengthen board and staff leadership, building a skill set of strategic thinking techniques for ongoing use
- create a clearer understanding of internal strengths and weaknesses and external opportunities and threats
- provide a context for decision-making that allows board and staff to evaluate multiple options and choose those that are most strategic
- help museum board and staff members to speak with a collective voice
- articulate a mission that drives all of the institution's work
- create a compelling vision that motivates internal and external stakeholders
- generate specific and measurable action steps to support the mission and achieve the vision.

Strategic planning is not easy. It creates change, which requires letting go of what is known and embracing what is unknown. A collaborative process builds the consensus and commitment that makes it possible to take this quantum leap. Strategic planning means choosing among competing priorities on many levels—from philosophical issues of mission and vision to operational issues of funding and facilities usage. A strong sense of mission and vision makes it possible to frame questions and find answers that are right for each institution.

The strategic thinking and planning process is organized in seven phases.

1. Plan to Plan
2. Clarify Mission, Vision, and Values
3. Scan the Environment
4. Determine Strategies
5. Develop Performance Measures
6. Develop Operating Plan and Budgets
7. Report and Monitor

Figure 0.14 shows how the seven phases flow into one another throughout the process. Although strategic planning is a sequential process that requires some phases to be completed before others are begun, the vertical stacking of the phases suggests that work on one phase can happen concurrently with another. For example, the environmental scan can begin while the museum's mission is being clarified.

The three horizontal bands indicate the general allocation of responsibility between board and staff. The precise allocation of effort will vary depending on the size of the board and staff and the institutional culture, but certain phases of the process fall more naturally within the domain of governance and others within the realm of management. Board and staff members as well as external stakeholders will be involved throughout the planning process, but Phase 2 (Clarify Mission, Vision, and Values) and Phase 5 (Develop Performance Measures), which appear in the top band, fall within the purview of the board; Phase 3 (Scan the Environment) and Phase 6

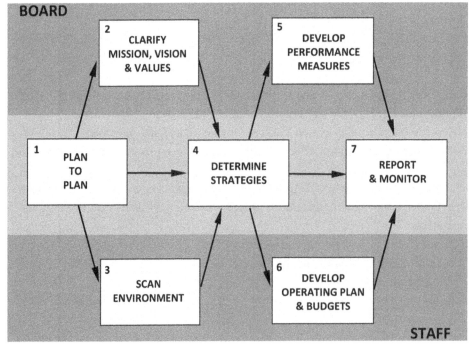

FIGURE 0.14
Seven Phases of Strategic Planning (Courtesy of the Museum Trustee Association)

(Develop Operating Plan and Budgets), which appear in the bottom band, are the primary responsibility of staff, though board and community members can play a vital role in the environmental scan. Phase 1 (Plan to Plan), Phase 4 (Determine Strategies), and Phase 7 (Report and Monitor), located in the middle of the chart, require shared responsibility and decision-making.

DIVERGENT AND CONVERGENT THINKING

Strategic planning calls for different types of thinking at different stages of the process. At the beginning, during Phases 1–3, the goal is to increase the Strategic Planning Team's understanding of the resources available to the museum, learn more about the perceptions of various external constituencies, understand the needs of current and future visitors, and expand the scope of possibilities. These stages require *divergent thinking*, gathering an ever-increasing array of data into the strategic thinking mix. Divergent thinking branches out in many directions to encompass any information that might be relevant. The goal is not to evaluate that information or identify what's most important but to arrive at the widest possible range of options.

Midway through the process—during Phase 4 (Determine Strategies)—the emphasis shifts to focusing, analyzing, and prioritizing the possibilities that have the greatest potential to move the museum forward. This emphasis calls for *convergent thinking*, which will be needed from this point forward. Convergent thinking draws together a variety of information and determines which is most relevant. The goal is to analyze, sort, and prioritize information to identify the strategic possibilities. Figure 0.15 shows the key tasks that fall within each of the seven phases. Phases that require divergent thinking are shaded in light gray, and those that require convergent thinking are in dark gray.

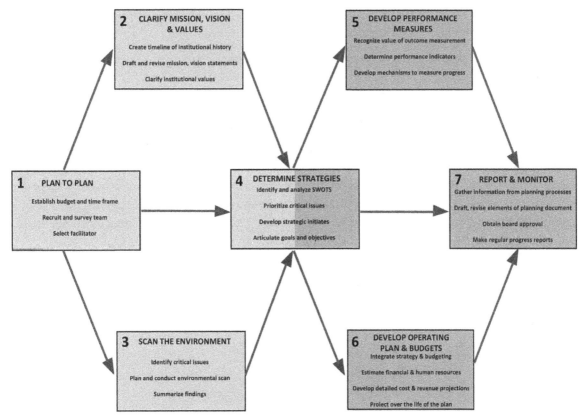

FIGURE 0.15
Key Tasks in Seven Phases (Courtesy of the Museum Trustee Association)

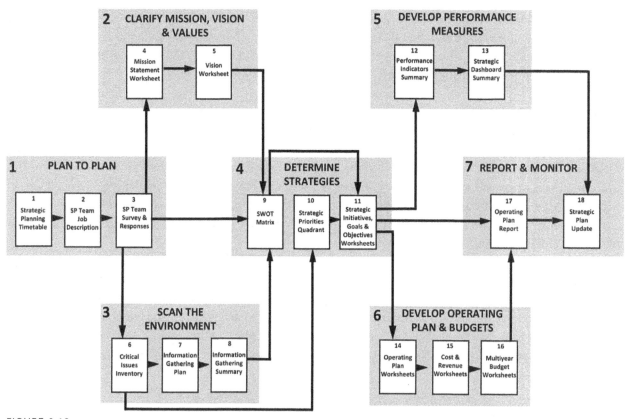

FIGURE 0.16
Templates Used in Seven Phases (Courtesy of the Museum Trustee Association)

Figure 0.16 shows the seven phases and the templates used in each phase. Although the planning process is sequential, it is not strictly linear, as the arrows connecting different templates show. For example, **Template 3: Strategic Planning Team Survey** informs **Template 6: Critical Issues Inventory**. The Critical Issues Inventory, in turn, informs **Template 7: Information-Gathering Plan** and **Template 10: Strategic Priorities Quadrant**. There is a constant interplay of well-known facts and fresh insights, both of which are woven into the planning process. At the same time that a particular phase builds upon those that precede it, it may be influenced by those that follow, making it necessary to revisit previous steps. Due to the iterative nature of the process, it is not at all unusual to take one step forward and two steps backward. The Strategic Planning Team should focus on maintaining its momentum, even when referring back to its work in previous phases.

Acknowledgments

John Adkins's thirty years of experience with technology includes writing apps for Fortune 500 companies. His knowledge and experience helped move *Templates for Trustees* into the twenty-first century with the introduction of the online app that is an integral part of each volume in this series. We are grateful for his creativity and persistence, which met every challenge we encountered in implementing this new platform.

The Museum Trustee Association and the authors thank Lawrence Butler, coauthor of the first edition of *Strategic Thinking and Planning*, for his strategic insights on nonprofit institutions and for his continued interest in this resource.

We also thank Gail Anderson for sharing her expertise on museum mission statements and for her bold thinking about the challenges that museums face in serving our nation's changing population.

The Institute of Museum and Library Services, a federal agency that fosters innovation, leadership, and a lifetime of learning, helped support the publication of the first edition of *Strategic Thinking and Planning*.

The Museum Trustee Association gratefully acknowledges the following donors whose support made the revision of this series possible:

The Wieler Family Foundation in honor of Mary Baily Wieler and Emily Inglis
Georgina T. and Thomas A. Russo
Margaret and Bill Benjamin
Andrew L. and Gayle Shaw Camden
Richard and Mary Kelly
Maureen Pecht King
Janis and William Wetsman Foundation
Kristine and Leland Peterson
Katherine Duff Rines
Murray R. Tarnapoll

Introduction

A New Approach to a Familiar Exercise

Many museum trustees and directors see strategic planning as one of their primary interests and concerns. As one board member put it, "Strategic planning is the essence of survival." The American Alliance of Museums (AAM) identifies a written strategic plan as one of five core documents that are fundamental to professional museum operations, embodying a museum's core values and practices. Yet *Museum Board Leadership 2017: A National Report*, commissioned by AAM, found that only 77 percent of museums have written strategic plans, as compared with 84 percent of other nonprofits.[1] Perhaps this is because creating a strategic plan requires such a big investment of time and energy on the part of board and staff leaders faced with priorities that are seemingly more urgent. Those who make this investment find that it pays off in the development of new attitudes and skills that stretch and strengthen both arms of leadership.

In looking beyond their own interests, experiences, and acquaintances, trustees gain a clearer understanding of perspectives in the larger community. In doing so, they can become staunch advocates for the needs of external stakeholders. With a keen interest in learning from the process, directors can suspend their tendency to lead the process and assume the role of active participants. The concept of servant leadership calls for a shift from "traditional autocratic and hierarchical modes of leadership" to a "combination of teamwork and community, personal involvement in decision making, and ethical and caring behavior."[2]

Strategic planning is not always a smooth, predictable, linear progression, but rather a creative process that requires a supple mindset. The destination is far more important than the specific route. It has been said that a strategic plan is more of a compass than a roadmap. So planning team members should resist the temptation to identify solutions before they have established the strategic initiatives. Even then, they should try to think in terms of general goals rather than concrete objectives—and, when it comes to process, to think of the "how" as well as the "what."

Typically, strategic plans are rewritten every three to five years. Writing a new plan or reviewing and revising an existing plan are critical exercises for board and staff leadership, but what happens in the meantime? Often the creative thinking required to craft a strategic plan is put on the back burner once a plan is developed and approved. The data gathering, analysis, imagination, and invention that go into strategic planning are ways of thinking that are always needed in nonprofit governance. Strategic *planning* may be an occasional event; strategic *thinking* should be an ongoing process for board and staff leadership—hence its inclusion in the title of this volume. In fact, strategic thinking should begin before and extend after the strategic planning process. It calls for prioritizing, discriminating, seeing connections, choosing among competing options, and always reflecting back on the mission and vision to measure alignment between the "what" and the "why." These kinds of thinking require a spirit of curiosity, open-mindedness, invention, and rigor.

Tom Peters and Robert Waterman, authors of *In Search of Excellence*, identify "simultaneous loose-tight properties" as one of the basic principles of exceptional management.[3] The most successful companies are rigidly governed by deeply held values but flexibly managed to allow for autonomy and innovation. What museum planning teams can learn from this principle is to stay tight on ends but loose on means. To be tight on ends, the board must build a strong commitment to the mission and vision of the institution. To be loose on means, it must allow staff members and other stakeholders to creatively adapt the methods to achieve these goals.

Museum directors and board chairs who responded to the *Museum Board Leadership 2017* survey gave their boards a grade of B- for their ability to think strategically.[4] This score, while acceptable, shows room for improvement. Mental, as well as physical, activities improve with practice, and the Strategic Planning Team will be introduced to several exercises designed to develop their strategic thinking "muscles" in the online app and in the pages that follow. New ways of thinking geared to the strategic planning process can also be helpful when decisions need to be made regarding other complex issues.

1. *Practice divergent and convergent thinking.* At the beginning of the process, team members will be encouraged to think broadly about the purpose and future of the museum without concern for the practical implications. This divergent thinking style is designed to open up the range of possibilities. Later, they will be asked to rank these issues and opportunities in a convergent style that leads to the identification of strategic initiatives, goals, and objectives.
2. *Maximize the potential of SWOTs.* A well-known technique for making the transition from divergent to convergent thinking involves the identification of strengths, weaknesses, opportunities, and threats, or SWOTs. The team will be introduced to four strategic thinking "operations" that expand on the SWOT paradigm, laying the groundwork for the strategic plan.
3. *Balance significance and urgency.* Strategic thinking calls for choosing among competing issues. **Template 10: Strategic Priorities Quadrant** and **Template 6: Critical Issues Inventory** will ask the team to prioritize critical issues in terms of their relative significance and urgency. These exercises will help identify the issues that call for strategic action.
4. *Integrate strategy and budget.* Because strategic thinking must be rooted in the reality of available resources, the team will be asked to "reality test" the strategic initiatives that emerge from the exercises by aligning them with the human, physical, and financial resources required to implement them. This activity will embed strategic thinking into the operational life of the institution.
5. *Monitor performance.* Respondents to the *Museum Board Leadership 2017* study gave their boards a C- for monitoring the performance and impact of strategic plans.[5] The tremendous investment of time, energy, and creativity on the parts of board, staff, and community members who work together to create a strategic plan clearly warrant effective, ongoing techniques for measuring progress. That is why the Strategic Planning Team will be challenged to define meaningful metrics and assessment approaches so the achievement of institutional mission as well as strategic initiatives, goals, and objectives can be monitored effectively.

While the strategic plan will guide the museum for the next few years, strategic thinking can inform the decision-making process of board and staff members on a daily basis, now and for decades to come. It can also help the museum to navigate the unexpected storms that come up in our increasingly dynamic and uncertain environment. No matter how forward looking the strategic plan, the museum may find itself in an unpredictable and sometimes threatening operating environment, and it must be able to respond strategically. The old adage

"You can't control what happens, but you can control how you respond to it" applies to institutions as well as individuals. Flexibility is so critical to an effective strategic plan that some institutions prefer the terms *strategic framework* or *strategic roadmap*.

The seven-stage planning process outlined in this publication will stimulate new ways of thinking strategically about the environment in which the institution operates and identifying the most strategic responses. This process employs eighteen templates. Some, like **Template 1: Strategic Planning Timetable** and **Template 7: Information-Gathering Plan**, will help the Strategic Planning Team organize and conduct the planning process. Others will continue to be useful to board and staff members long after the strategic plan is developed. For example, **Template 13: Strategic Dashboard Framework** will help monitor performance indicators on a regular basis. **Template 15: Cost and Revenue Worksheets** will help integrate the results of strategic planning into ongoing budgeting and financial planning. Each of these templates is a framework designed to be tailored to the specific needs of individual museums and the communities they serve.

THE CHARACTERISTICS OF AN EFFECTIVE STRATEGIC PLANNING PROCESS

The acronym CHOICES will help to remind Strategic Planning Team members of the qualities of an effective planning process:

- *Communication.* Information is shared rather than guarded in a process characterized by transparency. Cross-reporting among individuals and task forces will facilitate communication within the Strategic Planning Team. An informal monthly or bimonthly planning blog or e-newsletter can keep board and staff members who are not on the team in the loop.
- *Humor.* Lighten up! Humor makes the hard work and the challenging decisions rewarding. As one board member put it, "This is much too important to take too seriously!"
- *Openness.* Establish a climate characterized by candor, honesty, and dialogue rather than debate. Respecting and honoring opinions that are different from the norm will create comfort—even in the face of disagreement and risk taking—and may well lead to new discoveries.
- *Inclusiveness.* Involve all necessary perspectives—internal and external. The more inclusive the process, the more strategic the product. The more stakeholders involved in the process, the greater the buy-in. The more perspectives incorporated in a strategic plan, the greater its credibility.
- *Consensus building.* All team members need to feel invested in the outcomes of the process. Give everyone a vital role to play, whether in gathering, presenting, and analyzing the information, shaping the direction, or reviewing the draft. The goal is to develop deep ownership of mission, vision, critical issues, and strategies. An indicator that consensus is achieved is when team members speak about the plan and the process in the first person.
- *Energy.* Inertia is a powerful force, so involve people actively from the beginning to the end of the process. Asking team members to report to the group builds enthusiasm for the work that's being done. Incorporating individual and small-group exercises in meetings keeps everyone involved—even those who don't tend to speak out. Establishing and meeting deadlines keeps the momentum building.
- *Shared work.* The strategic planning process cannot depend on just a few people, no matter how bright and committed they are. It must include representatives of all departments across the institution so their specific areas of responsibility and expertise can all be considered and factored in. Each member's contributions have equal potential to influence the outcome of the strategic plan. Everyone who agrees to serve on the Strategic Planning Team must honor their commitment to participate actively throughout the planning process.

With this understanding of the characteristics of an effective strategic planning process, the allocation of board and staff effort, and the types of thinking, perspectives, and skills that are needed on the Strategic Planning Team, it's time to make concrete plans.

NOTES

1. BoardSource, *Museum Board Leadership 2017: A National Report* (Washington, DC: BoardSource, 2017), 19.

2. Michael Cardone Jr., *Business with Soul: Creating a Workplace Rich in Faith and Values* (Nashville, TN: Thomas Nelson, 2009), 68.

3. Thomas J. Peters and Robert H. Waterman Jr., *In Search of Excellence: Lessons from America's Best-Run Companies* (New York: Harper and Row, 1982), 318.

4. BoardSource, *Museum Board Leadership 2017*, 19.

5. Ibid.

Phase I

Plan to Plan

In the same way that no one would set out on a road trip without a final destination, some resting points along the way, a map, and a GPS device, a planning team shouldn't embark on a strategic planning process without forethought and familiarity with helpful tools. Most of the work outlined in this phase occurs before the first meeting and will determine the success of the entire process. After gaining a clear sense of the steps that will be involved, the board, the director, and others responsible for planning and facilitating the process will make critical decisions as they identify the key players; outline responsibilities for members of the board, the staff, and the Strategic Planning Team; and decide whether to hire a consultant as a facilitator. In short, this chapter lays the groundwork for the entire strategic planning process. Three templates are used in this phase:

- **Template 1: Strategic Planning Timetable** will help the team schedule the seven stages within the time allotted.
- **Template 2: Strategic Planning Team Job Description** will clarify what is required of internal and external stakeholders who are recruited to serve on the team.
- **Template 3: Strategic Planning Team Survey** is an online questionnaire to get each team member's feedback on critical issues that will be addressed in the strategic plan.
- **Report 3: Strategic Planning Team Responses** is automatically tabulated as team members respond to the survey.

Although the process must be carefully thought out to ensure that it includes all relevant stakeholders and addresses all key issues, it must be flexible enough to allow for synergy and unforeseen opportunities that present themselves. So while Strategic Planning Team leaders must plan to plan, they must also be agile enough to revise the plan as circumstances dictate and flexible enough to circle back in order to incorporate new information.

TAKE THE TIME TO DO IT RIGHT

Working with the chair of the Strategic Planning Team, the administrator will complete **Template 1: Strategic Planning Timetable**, creating a calendar that corresponds to the planning schedule. This template has two parts: a data entry worksheet and the timetable it generates. The data entry worksheet includes a button on the menu bar, "Adjust Start Date," where the administrator will insert the date the process will begin. Column 1 lists the seven phases; column 2 numbers the steps in each phase; and column 3 spells out each task and lists the relevant templates. Column 4 will be filled in by the administrator, who will indicate the number of days estimated for each task. The running number of days for each task will be calculated in column 5. The administrator can also add activities that might influence the planning process, such as visits to other museums, a focus group, or a board retreat.

TEMPLATE 1: STRATEGIC PLANNING TIMETABLE

	Step #	Task	Begins on Day	Days Duration
Phase 1:	1	Secure commitment of board and staff leadership	1	7
Plan to Plan	2	Identify Strategic Planning Team chair	7	7
	3	Establish budget for planning process	14	7
	4	Secure funding	21	14
	5	Select facilitator	21	14
	6	Establish time frame, milestones, meeting dates using **Template 1: Strategic Planning Timetable**	35	7
	7	Identify perspectives needed on Strategic Planning Team (SPT)	35	7
	8	Recruit SPT members using **Template 2: Strategic Planning Team Job Description**	42	14
	9	Review, assess past strategic planning processes	42	7
	10	Gather feedback from SPT members using **Template 3: Strategic Planning Team Survey**	56	7
Phase 2: Clarify Mission,	11	Discuss perspectives of team members using **Report 3: Strategic Planning Team Responses**	63	14
Vision, and	12	Create timeline of institutional history	63	14
Values	13	Consider the importance of mission and assess current mission statement	77	14
	14	Draft and revise mission statement using **Template 4: Mission Statement Worksheet**	77	14
	15	Draft and revise vision statement using **Template 5: Vision Statement Worksheet**	77	14
	16	Clarify institutional values and create values statement, if called for	77	14
Phase 3:	17	Collect critical issues using **Template 6: Critical Issues Inventory**	91	7
Scan the Environment	18	Plan environmental scan using **Template 7: Information-Gathering Plan**	91	7
	19	Conduct environmental scan	98	21
	20	Apply findings using **Template 8: Information-Gathering Summary**	119	14
	21	Identify trends and needs for additional information	119	14
	22	Expand scope of environmental scan as needed	119	14
Phase 4:	23	Use SWOTs as the basis for strategic thinking using **Template 9: SWOT Matrix**	133	14
Determine Strategies	24	Prioritize critical issues using **Template 10: Strategic Priorities Quadrant**	133	14
	25	Develop strategic initiatives using **Template 11A: Strategic Initiatives Worksheet**	147	14

	Step #	Task	Begins on Day	Days Duration
	26	Identify goals and objectives using **Template 11B: Goals and Objectives Worksheet**	147	14
	27	Consider changes to current operations to free up resources for new initiatives	147	14
Phase 5: Develop Performance Measures	28	Consider the value and challenges of outcome measurement	161	14
	29	Collect and examine examples of performance indicators	161	14
	30	Think strategically about performance indicators using **Template 12: Performance Indicators Inventory**	161	14
	31	Develop mechanisms to report on achievement of strategic initiatives using **Template 13: Strategic Dashboard Framework**	175	14
Phase 6: Develop Operating Plan and Budgets	32	Consider the importance of integrating strategy and budgeting	175	14
	33	Estimate financial and human resources of strategic initiatives using **Template 14: Operating Plan Worksheets**	175	14
	34	Develop detailed cost and revenue projections using **Template 15: Cost and Revenue Worksheets**	189	14
	35	Project costs and revenues over the life of the plan using **Template 16: Multiyear Budget Worksheets**	189	14
Phase 7: Report and Monitor	36	Gather necessary information for strategic planning document	203	14
	37	Consider the various audiences and purposes of the document	203	14
	38	Draft planning document and circulate to Strategic Planning Team for review	217	21
	39	Incorporate feedback in final draft	238	7
	40	Obtain board support and approval	245	14
	41	Establish a task force to oversee implementation of the plan	245	14
	42	Develop mechanism for regular progress reports using **Template 17: Operating Plan Report**	259	14
	43	Report on achievement of strategic initiatives using **Template 18: Strategic Plan Update**	273	ongoing
	44	Revise board operations and agendas to focus on strategic issues	273	ongoing

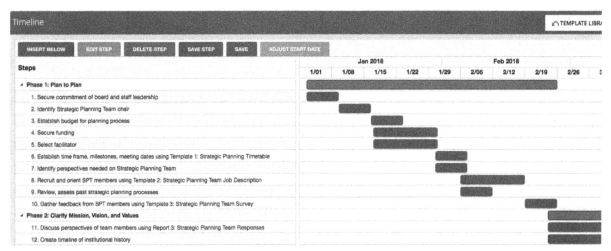

FIGURE 1.1
Strategic Planning Timetable (Courtesy of the Museum Trustee Association)

As the administrator enters data in the app, a timeline is automatically generated showing the approximate amount of time required to accomplish each task. The timeline will reflect any changes made to the schedule. It can be printed and distributed to the Strategic Planning Team at the start of the planning process and modified at various points along the way to update the team on its progress.

Figure 1.1 is an illustration of the timeline generated by the above data entry worksheet. It outlines a process that extends over a nine-month period, assuming that the Strategic Planning Team will meet approximately every two weeks.

Depending upon the time and resources available, a museum may take either a quick and somewhat condensed approach or a more thorough and extended approach to developing its strategic plan. In either case, it's important to work through all seven stages, though some can be condensed. For example, the time to complete an environmental scan can be shortened through the use of online surveys rather than one-on-one interviews. An abbreviated approach would not skip any steps; it would simply fit them into a shorter period.

Time permitting, a nine-to-twelve-month time frame is optimal. But if all seven stages must be condensed into a six-month strategic planning process, board and staff task forces can be working simultaneously on different phases. For example, after working together to plan and launch the process in months 1 and 2, board members can take the lead in articulating the mission during month 3, while staff members gather information in the environmental scan. The two groups can come together in month 4 to determine strategies; then, in months 5 and 6, board members can establish performance indicators and a broad-brush budget while staff members set to work on developing the details of the operating plan and projecting it out through the life of the strategic plan.

Today some institutions aim to develop strategic plans that are briefer and more concise in response to current thinking about attention span in light of the vast amount of information we encounter on a daily basis. Less may well be more when it comes to the length of the written plan; however, a shorter planning process does not necessarily lead to a shorter planning document. In fact, the opposite may be true. Often, additional time to process findings brings additional clarity to the strategic thinking process.

THE BOARD'S RESPONSIBILITIES FOR STRATEGIC PLANNING

Strategic planning deserves a place at the top of the board's list of priorities. In the words of John Carver, "The most important work of any governing board is to create and re-create the reason for organizational existence." Not a task that is done once, and then forgotten, "it is a perpetual obligation, deserving of the majority of board time and energy."[1] Not every board member will serve on the Strategic Planning Team; some do not have active roles to play in the process. The full board should be involved in the following steps:

- Reviewing the current strategic plan and having a conversation about whether it still serves as a guiding light for the board's work.
- Suggesting what internal and external perspectives are needed in the strategic planning process and suggesting individuals who can provide those perspectives. The links that board members provide to the museum's external constituencies are a valuable contribution to the planning process.
- Offering feedback as requested by the Strategic Planning Team. For example, the board may be asked to review a draft of the mission statement.
- Approving the final plan, which requires the board's enthusiastic support as well as its formal approval.
- Taking responsibility for ensuring that strategic goals and objectives are realized. In keeping with their fiduciary responsibility, board members are bound to ensure that the museum has the necessary financial resources and to hold the museum accountable for realizing its mission.
- Monitoring the effectiveness of the plan on a regular basis. The best way to guarantee this ongoing review is to build the strategic plan into regular board routines, such as budgeting and performance reviews, and use it to shape strategic agendas for board meetings.[2] The director and others in leadership positions should be held accountable for the goals outlined in the strategic plan.

In addition to these responsibilities, some boards may assume a more hands-on role throughout the process. In terms of allocation of effort, there are three models of strategic planning, each with a different level of board involvement that will suit institutions with different needs and resources.

In a *board-driven process*, the board chair, other board leaders, and members of critical committees form an ad hoc task force to lead the strategic planning process. The board works with the director and other key staff members to gather internal reports that show trends in attendance, membership, and finances as well as external data that show trends in the community. Together, board and staff leaders identify critical issues and develop strategic goals. With input from stakeholders, staff members develop specific strategies to achieve these goals. Start-up museums or smaller museums with a limited number of professional staff members might take this approach to create their strategic plan.

In a *staff-driven process*, the director and members of his or her executive team provide the impetus for strategic planning. They identify key board and staff members with whom they will work on developing a plan and accompanying budget, which will be presented to the full board for review and approval. For this approach to be successful, board input must be sought at critical stages and given careful consideration. One advantage of this model is that it can be accomplished in a relatively short time. This approach might be appropriate in a national organization with a board that meets quarterly.

In a *participatory process*, the broadest possible involvement is sought from internal and external constituencies. An inclusive approach, like the one recommended in this book, shares responsibility among board and staff members, as well as external stakeholders who will be affected by the plan or play a part in its implementation. The director and the board chair (or Executive Committee) work together to plan the process and recruit the Strategic Planning Team. Drawing on each of their connections and networks, team members participate in an environmental scan and share information necessary to identify critical issues. The team may form task forces to draft the mission, vision, and values statements, create budgets, develop action plans, and set up systems for monitoring progress. Although a participatory process requires a considerable amount of time and energy, it pays off in a plan that addresses the larger community's needs and builds a broad sense of ownership and commitment.

THE ROLE OF THE STRATEGIC PLANNING TEAM

The Strategic Planning Team is the group charged with articulating the mission and vision; identifying strategic initiatives, goals, and objectives for the future; and developing a plan to achieve them. This group may be an ad hoc group specially convened to develop the strategic plan, or it may be a standing committee of the board augmented by staff members and other stakeholders. In either case, it is critical to include participants with a broad range of perspectives. There is nothing strategic about sitting around the table with a group of people who share the same opinions and points of view and everything to gain by widening the circle. The strategic planning process is an opportunity for the museum to implement participatory and democratic ways of working that are intentionally visitor and community centered. Decentralizing information gathering and decision-making and promoting broader collaboration can lead to institutions that are more innovative, agile, and likely to have a shared purpose with all stakeholders in the "human ecosystem."[3]

For planning to be strategic, the planning team must incorporate the perspectives of internal and external stakeholders. Internal stakeholders include board members, staff members (at various levels of the organizational structure), and volunteers. External stakeholders include members, donors, teachers, community partners, neighborhood groups, funders, and perhaps experts in the museum's discipline. Special types of museums must also consider their unique constituencies. For example, university museums will need to incorporate the perspectives of faculty members, administrators, students, and alumni. Municipal or state museums will need to involve city or state government officials.

In addition to various perspectives, certain skill sets are needed on the Strategic Planning Team. One is facilitation—the ability to encourage participation and draw out the best thinking from a diverse group of individuals. Communication and record keeping are other important skill sets that will be needed when it comes to collecting and summarizing data generated by the Strategic Planning Team and community members. These critical functions will be required throughout the strategic planning process. They may be carried out by a consultant, the director, a board member, or the strategic planning administrator.

KEY PLAYERS ON THE TEAM

In the same way that each member of a winning team plays a particular position and sees the game from that vantage point, each member of the Strategic Planning Team brings different strengths, connections, and perspectives. Their relationship with the museum dictates the position they will play. Each stakeholder—internal and external—contributes to the effectiveness of the whole team.

In many aspects of museum leadership, either the board chair or the director may take the lead. But in strategic planning, both arms of governance have equally valuable perspectives to bring to the table. This shared responsibility represents one of the most valuable and challenging aspects of the strategic thinking and planning process. And because the next generation of leaders is often the ones who wind up implementing the plan, it makes sense to invite board vice chairs and committee heads to join the Strategic Planning Team.

As chief executive and staff liaison, the *director* plays a critical role on the Strategic Planning Team. He or she is in the best position to

- create the impetus for the process and build staff buy-in
- provide data on current programs and services

- share information about current and upcoming exhibitions and programs
- encourage strategic thinking at all levels of the organizational structure by linking the strategic plan to departmental and individual work plans
- ensure that the budget is linked to the strategic initiatives outlined in the plan
- establish standards that reflect best practices in the profession

As board leader, the *board chair* is in the best position to

- keep the full board apprised on the planning process
- bring mission and vision statements to the board for approval (but not wordsmithing)
- solicit feedback on key issues identified in the environmental scan
- involve the vice chair and other up-and-coming leaders, as they will likely be involved in implementing the plan

As those with fiduciary responsibility for the institution, *board members-at-large* are in a position to

- approach issues from a big-picture perspective
- connect with stakeholders and supporters in the larger community
- prioritize the many—and sometimes competing—options available to the museum
- offer expertise in needed nonmuseum disciplines
- ensure that adequate resources are available to realize the strategic plan

As the museum's arms into the community, *external stakeholders* can

- contribute outside perspectives not clearly understood by staff and board members
- provide feedback based on a broader, external perspective rather than the detailed point of view of insiders
- make connections with the diverse constituencies they represent
- serve as ambassadors for the museum, translating its mission and vision to their respective communities
- make important contributions to the overall shape and direction of the plan even if they are not official members of the Strategic Planning Team

The *facilitator* who will lead the Strategic Planning Team plays a key role in the process. (See p. 14 for a discussion of the benefits of hiring a consultant to facilitate the planning process.) The role of an outside facilitator is generally made clear, and if a staff or board member fills this role, clarity about roles is especially important. The facilitator cannot lead the planning process and be a participant in it.

The *administrator*, who manages the flow of information, schedules meetings, and keeps the process organized, will work hand in hand with the facilitator and board leadership.

SELECTING THE STRATEGIC PLANNING TEAM

The selection of Strategic Planning Team members is one of the most critical steps in the entire planning process. The individuals who are chosen—their perspectives, experience, and connections—will be the catalysts for change in the institution. They will shape the museum's mission and articulate its vision, identify and prioritize critical issues, and develop strategic initiatives that will guide the museum for the next several years.

The leaders of the planning team should make a list of the various perspectives that are needed, and then identify one or more individuals who can provide them. Those who represent multiple perspectives—the teacher who is also a parent or the donor who serves on the board of another local nonprofit institution—will be especially valuable additions to the team. The director, board chair, and Strategic Planning Team chair should have a thoughtful conversation about each person who is being considered, looking not only for individual contributions but also for the mix of perspectives on the team as a whole. It's helpful to make a list of individuals who should definitely be on the team and a backup list of others to contact if the first choices are not available. If individuals with critical perspectives are unable to serve, ask them to recommend someone else.

Consider how each stakeholder's perspective could best be incorporated into the overall process. Those whose input will be needed throughout the process should be appointed to the Strategic Planning Team. Those who have specific pieces to contribute to the puzzle can be involved at key points, such as during the environmental scan or the review of drafts. Individuals who are not members of the Strategic Planning Team can also be invited to attend selected meetings to contribute their perspectives and expertise. It's not unusual for someone who is not officially a member of the Strategic Planning Team to share an insight or contribute an idea that becomes a key part of the plan.

Give careful consideration to the optimum size of the team, which will be influenced by the number of perspectives needed and the culture of the institution. Some boards are comfortable investing small groups with the responsibility to make big decisions, while others favor a more broad-based and participatory process. To have a critical mass at meetings and a corps of people who can share assignments, somewhere between eight and twelve members is a good range. Any more than that can become unwieldy, making it difficult to schedule meetings and maintain momentum and continuity. Bear in mind practical considerations, such as the time available for each meeting. Larger teams will bring more perspectives to bear, but the more people there are at the table, the longer it will take for all voices to be heard. It's important that everyone be given the opportunity to participate actively in meetings. Sometimes smaller groups inspire more active participation.

SECURING THE COMMITMENT OF STRATEGIC PLANNING TEAM MEMBERS
Serving on the Strategic Planning Team constitutes a valuable contribution to the institution. It requires a serious commitment of time, thought, and energy from the start of the process to the end. Those approaching prospective team members should stress the value of their contribution and make the expectations as clear and specific as possible from the very beginning. **Template 2: Strategic Planning Team Job Description** articulates the team's purpose and outlines the responsibilities and expectations of members. Don't underestimate the amount of time that will be required in order to get the agreement of prospective members; if they are told that the process won't require much of their time, they won't be prepared to give much. But if the importance of the plan to the future of the institution is made clear, they are more likely to give their active and sustained participation. This commitment is especially important in an iterative process where each meeting builds upon the previous meetings and leads to the next. Team members who drop in and out of the process will not be able to contribute effectively.

While board and staff members will have a history with the museum, external stakeholders will appreciate a packet of information to orient them. Some will be familiar with the institution, but others may not be aware of its history or its most recent initiatives. An orientation packet—printed or electronic—should be compiled for the entire team so that participants have everything in one place and all are starting on the same page. It might include the following material:

- a roster of Strategic Planning Team members with addresses, phone numbers, and e-mail addresses
- the current mission statement and related documents, such as vision or values statements

TEMPLATE 2: STRATEGIC PLANNING TEAM JOB DESCRIPTION

{[Museum Name]}
{[Mission Statement]}

Purpose

- Relying on a team process of information gathering and strategic thinking, the Strategic Planning Team will draft a strategic plan that will guide the museum's [insert words and phrases re: priorities] for the next [number] to [number] years.
- This ad hoc committee will be in place until a new strategic plan is presented to and approved by the board, a period estimated to be [number] to [number] months.

Membership

- The process will be guided by [insert name of individual or firm], [a consultant/an in-house facilitator/a community facilitator], with experience in [insert brief description of facilitator's background].
- The team will include [number] to [number] members, which may include board and staff members, as well as volunteers, institutional partners, and community members.
- Ex officio members may include [insert titles and associations].

Responsibilities

- Complete a brief online survey prior to the first meeting of the Strategic Planning Team to take the pulse of the group.
- Attend [weekly/biweekly/monthly/periodic] meetings of the Strategic Planning Team expected to begin in [month] and end in [month].
- Assess the relevance of the current mission statement and revise or rewrite, as needed.
- Evaluate the need for vision, values, or other foundational statements and create, as needed.
- Participate in an environmental scan to gather information from community stakeholders and report on findings.
- Identify and prioritize strategic issues, establish goals and objectives, and develop ways to monitor progress.

Expectations

- Maintain confidentiality throughout the strategic planning process, relying on the Strategic Planning Team Chair to communicate progress with internal and external stakeholders.
- Participate actively in all Strategic Planning Team meetings, joining remotely if unable to meet in person.
- Familiarize yourself with the {[Museum Name]}'s history and current programs and envision new initiatives.

- the most recent strategic plan
- operating budgets for the current year and the two prior years
- annual reports for the past two years and final reports on special projects
- a chronology of the museum's history
- recent and pending grant applications
- audience research, such as focus groups, exit interviews, or member surveys
- selected newsletters and brochures
- staff roster with backgrounds and responsibilities
- board roster with backgrounds and responsibilities

CONSIDER HIRING A CONSULTANT TO FACILITATE THE PROCESS

Those involved in strategic planning must be able to see *both* the forest *and* the trees. The people who are most invested in an institution—board and staff members alike—are often so focused on the pressing demands of their particular roles that it's difficult to see beyond them. It's also extremely challenging to be objective about the place where one invests so much time, talent, and energy. An outside facilitator can:

- serve as a neutral third party, lending objectivity to a group that is inclined to feel passionately about the museum. A dispassionate outsider can more easily uncover and put on the table key issues that need to be addressed—issues that might be deemed too sensitive by those within the institution or have become "invisible" because they are so much a part of the institutional culture.
- provide a confidential sounding board to which board members can bring questions and concerns about governance and to which the director can bring questions and concerns about management. Skilled consultants are able to obtain sensitive information, hold it in confidence, and share it in constructive ways.
- free all parties—especially board and staff leaders—to participate fully without feeling that, because of their position or role, they should run the meetings or orchestrate the process. Anyone who has served as secretary knows how difficult it is to participate actively in a meeting while taking notes. Facilitating a strategic planning process demands far more in terms of listening carefully, ensuring everyone's participation, and staying one step ahead of the discussion.
- make the most of synergies by building consensus among stakeholders with differing points of view and seeing ways to organize ideas that may seem to be opposed or even contradictory.
- reflect on the process based on experience with a variety of other institutions. Knowing whether particular issues or aspects of the process are unique or typical can help determine how much time is worth investing in them.
- enforce discipline around the strategic planning work to ensure that key milestones are met and interim documents are created in a timely fashion.
- use various techniques to ensure that all voices are heard, drawing out those who are not inclined to speak.

Cost is, of course, a factor in deciding whether to hire a consultant and which one to choose. The cost for facilitating a strategic planning process can vary from a few thousand dollars for a solo practitioner who is locally or regionally based to tens of thousands for a large national firm. To those who may be inclined to think that consultants are too expensive, a nonprofit management consultant says, "Even spending a few months poorly is a very expensive undertaking when one thinks about how scarce the major resource of most organizations is: the time of staff and board members."[4]

If the museum decides to hire a consultant, it should look for someone who will respect differences of opinion, create synergy from different perspectives, synthesize many ideas, manage discussions so that everyone is heard, and make the best use of everyone's time. The team wants someone who will facilitate the process, not someone who will dictate the outcome of the plan. The impetus, inspiration, and implementation of the plan must come from within the institution and the communities it serves. Remember, the best facilitator is the one who asks the best questions. To find the right fit for the museum, the planning team should ask for recommendations from colleagues at other institutions, professional organizations, and funders, such as the local United Way or community foundation; solicit proposals; and then narrow the list to two or three finalists.

Case in point: One museum invited two finalists to come to the museum to meet with senior staff. This approach gave the consultants an opportunity to learn staff members' concerns and get a sense of their individual contributions as well as the institutional culture. It also gave board and staff members an opportunity to ask questions about the process and see how the two consultants thought on their feet. When the staff members debriefed after the meetings, they found that they were in complete agreement about which consultant would be the best fit. The selection process built a solid foundation for the working relationship between the staff and the consultant.

MAKING THE MOST OF STRATEGIC PLANNING TEAM MEETINGS

Considering the amount of time that each team member contributes and the depth of their experience and multiplying that by the number of team members suggests the tremendous resource seated around the table. To make the most of meetings, consider the following:

- What can best be accomplished in a large-group setting, and what can be done individually or in small groups?
- Are there some steps that would best be assigned to task forces headed by a Strategic Planning Team member and including other stakeholders from the board, staff, or community?
- What kinds of issues gain clarity when they are shared and discussed during meetings?
- What can be reported in writing and distributed before meetings?
- What issues require reflection and processing before a decision can be reached?
- When is it important for all team members to weigh in on a particular issue?
- How much can the team reasonably expect to accomplish in any given meeting?
- What are the best mechanisms for recording the team's responses and reporting on the meetings?

In the interest of consistency and continuity, someone who will be available at every meeting—preferably the administrator—should be asked to take minutes. If the museum has hired a consultant, they may prefer to do meeting minutes or notes as part of their scope of work. In an iterative process like strategic planning, minutes provide a valuable record of the evolution of the team's thinking. They should summarize what was accomplished at each meeting and outline what remains to be done, keeping these points in mind:

- Emphasize the decisions that were made, citing critical information that contributed to those decisions and perhaps listing its sources. Incorporate drafts of documents that were created, highlighting changes from one iteration to the next.
- Summarize the team's discussions succinctly, perhaps listing discussion points taken from flip charts, which can be recorded digitally.
- Remind people of individual and task force assignments and deadlines.
- List issues that require responses and unanswered questions that need to be resolved.
- In addition to minutes, be sure to distribute agendas well in advance of upcoming meetings.

The setting of Strategic Planning Team meetings will establish a tone for the dynamics of the group, the tenor of the discussions, the caliber of thinking, and the type of planning that results. Meeting off site has many advantages. Staff team members are better able to focus on priorities for the future when they are removed from the distractions and interruptions of their day-to-day responsibilities and the expectations to serve as troubleshooters or hosts. Off-site locations also have advantages for board members, who can assume a different role outside the familiar surroundings of the museum's boardroom. Conference facilities include many amenities for conducting large meetings and smaller breakout sessions, creature comforts for all participants, and food service facilities for breaks and meals.

The team may also want to consider the advantages of on-site meetings, which include cost savings and access to museum facilities. Planners can give the Strategic Planning Team the benefits of both settings by scheduling some meetings at the museum and other meetings off site.

BUDGETING FOR THE PLANNING PROCESS

Strategic Planning Team leaders should give focused and creative thought to all aspects of the planning budget. Like any process that involves numerous participants and multiple meetings, both direct costs and opportunity costs will be incurred. Direct costs might include such items as meeting rooms and audiovisual equipment rentals, refreshments and meals, consultant fees, and accommodations. If the museum elects to hire a planning consultant, it is wise to develop a budget and limit the search to firms that fit within those parameters. Colleagues at other museums or nonprofit organizations in the community can help museum leadership set realistic budgets and expectations. The environmental scan may incur costs for research and data analysis as well as potential travel to other museums. And there are always charges for copying, mailing, and editing services.

Opportunity costs are less obvious but no less important. They include the value of participants' time (board members, staff members, and other stakeholders) that might be spent in other ways. The longer the process lasts and the more it requires of participants, the more expensive it will be in terms of direct and indirect costs. But since these costs are an investment in the museum's future, weigh them carefully against the long-term benefits of a more extensive, broadly participatory planning process.

In addition to containing costs, look for ways to defray expenses through in-kind contributions or planning grants, which are often available from local foundations and other grant-making agencies. Planning often comes under the broad category of "capacity building" in grant guidelines.

LEARNING FROM PRIOR PLANS AND PLANNING PROCESSES

Most institutions have a previous strategic plan that has been implemented to a greater or lesser degree. Reviewing the most recent plan and the process that led to its creation can provide valuable information for the consultant or facilitator who is leading the current process. Though external circumstances may have changed considerably, chances are that the internal culture is similar. Interview veteran board members and, if feasible, previous directors to learn their perspectives on the strengths and weaknesses of previous planning efforts.

- Who facilitated the process? Was the facilitator's style a good fit with the culture of the institution?
- Was adequate time devoted to individual meetings and the process as a whole? If not, what wasn't addressed?
- Were all necessary perspectives included? If not, what perspectives were missing?
- What mechanisms were put in place to monitor progress on the plan, and which were most effective?
- How much of the plan was actually implemented?

GATHERING INITIAL IMPRESSIONS OF THE STRATEGIC PLANNING TEAM

It is important to get team members thinking about the strategic issues the museum faces even before the first meeting, which will be more productive if participants have already begun to reflect on their impressions of the institution and its place in the community.

Template 3: Strategic Planning Team Survey is an online survey for gathering the perspectives of team members. After meeting with the director and chair of the Strategic Planning Team, the administrator can customize the questions and response options on the survey to the museum's circumstances. They should send the link to the survey to all members of the Strategic Planning Team two weeks before the first meeting and ask that it be completed a week in advance. If broader participation is desired, the survey can be sent to all board members and staff leaders.

TEMPLATE 3: STRATEGIC PLANNING TEAM SURVEY

The Strategic Planning Team is composed of individuals with diverse perspectives on the museum. To help us incorporate many points of view in the planning process, please take a few minutes to complete this short survey. So that we can share the results at our first meeting on [date], please respond by [date].

1. Please check all of your current museum roles.

   Museum member
   Board member
   Staff member
   Volunteer
   Community member
   Donor

2. In thinking strategically about the future of the museum, please check all perspectives you bring to the process.

   Educator, elementary
   Educator, secondary
   Educator, college
   Parent of school-aged child(ren)
   Grandparent
   Neighborhood group
   Community organization

We must serve

3. To add value to our community the museum must serve . . . Please check your top five responses.

   adults
   families

school groups
youth
young adults
seniors
people who frequent museums
people who don't attend museums
people of color
local residents
tourists
other

4. The museum's greatest strengths are its . . . Please check your top five responses.

collection
building and grounds
location
size of museum/galleries
staff
board
volunteers
donors
research/scholarship
exhibits
programs
online resources
other uses of technology
visibility/marketing
internal communication
external communication
financial resources/sustainability
fundraising
accessibility
community support/participation
engagement with community
relevance to the community
collaborations/partnerships
history/traditions
reputation
other

5. The museum's five greatest weaknesses/challenges are its . . . Please check your top five responses.

collection
building and grounds
location
size of museum/galleries
staff
board
volunteers
donors
research/scholarship
exhibits
programs
online resources
other uses of technology
visibility/marketing
internal communication
external communication
financial resources/sustainability
fundraising
accessibility
community support/participation
engagement with community
relevance to the community
collaborations/partnerships
history/traditions
reputation
other

6. Looking ahead to the next three to five years, I think these three factors must be considered in thinking strategically about the future of the museum:

7. The museum exists to . . .

8. From my perspective, the museum will be sustainable if it continues on its current path.

Agree strongly
Agree
Disagree
Disagree strongly
No opinion

The administrator will be able to see who has completed the online survey so reminder emails can be sent to those who have not responded. As each team member completes the survey their responses will be compiled into **Report 3: Strategic Planning Team Survey Responses**. As responses are entered, graphs are created showing a profile of the roles and perspectives represented on the team and the team's responses.

Because questions 1 and 2 ask respondents to check all that apply, this hypothetical team of twelve includes many roles and perspectives on the museum. Figure 1.2 provides a picture of the ways team members, some of whom have multiple roles, are connected to the museum. For example, some board members are also donors.

This group of twelve also brings their perspectives as parents and grandparents, members of neighborhood groups and community organizations, and educators. Figure 1.3 shows the multiple perspectives they bring to the table, such as the grandparent who is also a university professor and a member of a neighborhood group.

Questions 3, 4, and 5 ask respondents to check their top five responses, which requires them to prioritize the many options listed. Figure 1.4 reveals that most team members see local residents as a higher priority than tourists when it comes to adding value to the community. The fact that eight of the twelve see people of color as a high priority suggests that these community members are, or have been, underserved. And while many team members would probably be inclined to choose the conventional museum audiences of families and elementary school groups, youth received an equal number of responses. This may be due to the fact that middle school and high school students are new and important audiences for museums and other community organizations to serve.

Since the same quality can be perceived as a strength by some and as a weakness by others, the twenty-five response options for questions 4 and 5 (figures 1.5 and 1.6) are identical. For example, the museum's reputation is seen as a strength by two team members who may value the prestige associated with the institution, and a weakness

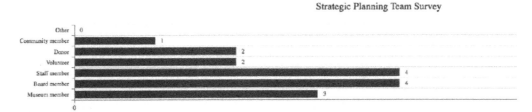

FIGURE 1.2
Strategic Planning Team Responses, Question 1 (Courtesy of the Museum Trustee Association)

FIGURE 1.3
Strategic Planning Team Responses, Question 2 (Courtesy of the Museum Trustee Association)

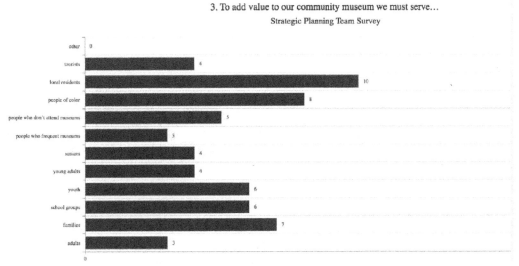

FIGURE 1.4

Strategic Planning Team Responses, Question 3 (Courtesy of the Museum Trustee Association)

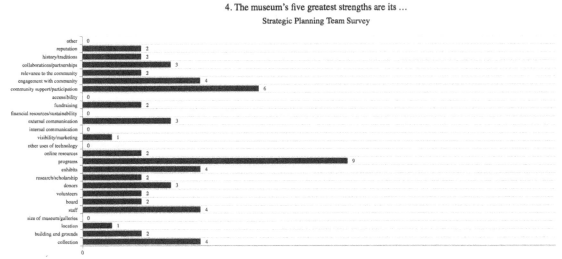

FIGURE 1.5

Strategic Planning Team Responses, Question 4 (Courtesy of the Museum Trustee Association)

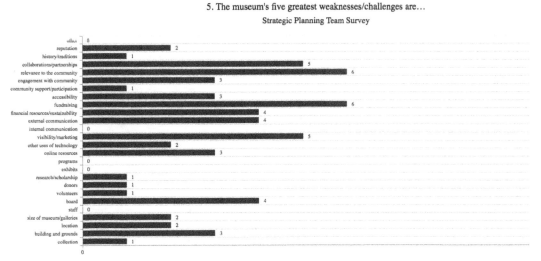

FIGURE 1.6

Strategic Planning Team Responses, Question 5 (Courtesy of the Museum Trustee Association)

by two others who may have opinions that it is living on past laurels. Three members identify collaborations and partnerships as a strength, while five count it as a weakness, perhaps because they see the need for more. The museum has been successful in building community support, suggested by the fact that six respondents identify it as a strength and only one as a weakness. Perhaps this stems from the quality of museum programs, seen as a strength by nine team members. As in many museums, fundraising is a proverbial challenge, as evidenced by the fact that six identify it as a weakness and only two as a strength. Two respondents see the board as a strength, while four perceive it as a weakness, perhaps recognizing the ongoing need for greater diversity and inclusion on museum boards. All of these differing views can generate meaningful dialogues in Strategic Planning Team meetings—dialogues that will ultimately lead to the creation of new strategic initiatives.

The answers to open-ended questions will be collected verbatim in separate reports. To analyze the responses, an individual or a small group of Strategic Planning Team members should look for common themes and group similar responses into broadly stated categories. The summary should list only those categories with three or more responses and include no more than five categories for each question. The point is not to record every response but to show consensus on key issues that are of strategic importance. Distribute the responses to both the multiple choice and the open-ended questions prior to the first meeting so team members can begin to process the findings. When they come together, they'll be able to see trends.

7. The museum exists to

Responses:

Use the permanent collection and temporary exhibitions to educate visitors and broaden their vision of possibilities

Promote an appreciation of art and art history

Provide public access to a distinguished art collection and educational programming

Provide a high quality art and cultural component to our rural community

Serve the community by offering a unique experience not otherwise available in our small town

Change our community. (A good museum serves its community; a great museum changes it.)

Demonstrate how exposure to the visual arts can be woven into everyone's daily lives

Enrich the cultural experiences of our community by exposing people to creations of the soul

Increase exposure to the visual arts to further the appreciation and understanding of many cultures

Educate the community through exhibits of original art and artifacts and actively engage their minds through programming

FIGURE 1.7
Strategic Planning Team Responses, Question 7 (Courtesy of the Museum Trustee Association)

For example, in exploring responses to the open-ended question "The museum exists to . . ." (figure 1.7), one museum's Strategic Planning Team members grouped quotes in several categories, including the following:

Educate, inform, and inspire

- Educate the community through exhibits of original art and artifacts and actively engage their minds through programming
- Promote an appreciation of art and art history
- Use the permanent collection and temporary exhibitions to educate visitors and broaden their vision of possibilities
- Demonstrate how exposure to the visual arts can be woven into everyone's daily lives
- Provide public access to a distinguished art collection and educational programming

Create public value for our community

- Increase exposure to the visual arts to further the appreciation and understanding of many cultures
- Provide a high-quality art and cultural component to our rural community
- Serve the community by offering a unique experience not otherwise available in our small town
- Enrich the cultural experiences of our community by exposing people to creations of the soul
- Change our community (a good museum serves its community; a great museum changes it)

The results of the Strategic Planning Team Survey will not only show the diverse perspectives represented on the team but also demonstrate that there is a foundation on which to build the strategic plan. Everyone must see their participation in the process from the beginning, so put a discussion of survey results on the agenda for the first meeting. The following questions will generate an interesting dialogue:

- In light of responses to question 7, is there clarity and consensus about the museum's purpose?
- Who does the museum need to serve with its exhibits, programs, and partnerships?
- Which of the many potential audiences are well served, and which must be better served?
- Is there consensus about the museum's greatest strengths? If not, do staff, board, and external constituencies have different views?
- What are the relationships between strengths and weaknesses?
- In light of question 6, what strategic issues are identified at this early stage of the process?

A well-chosen Strategic Planning Team comes to the process with much of the knowledge that is needed to identify the challenges and solutions that will be addressed in the strategic plan. At the end of the planning process, it is always interesting to look back to **Report 3: Strategic Planning Team Responses** and note how many of the issues identified there evolved into strategic initiatives.

NOTES

1. John Carver, *Boards That Make a Difference: A New Design for Leadership in Nonprofit and Public Organizations*, 2nd ed. (San Francisco: Jossey-Bass, 1997), 50.

2. See *Building Museum Boards*, pp. 5–7, for a description of strategic board agendas and their impact.

3. Mike Murawski, "Towards a More Human-Centered Museum: Part 1, Rethinking Hierarchies," *Art Museum Teaching*, January 22, 2018, https://artmuseumteaching.com/2018/01/22/rethinking-hierarchies/.

4. Mike Allison, "In Defense of Strategic Planning: A Rebuttal," accessed March 12, 2018, http://www.blueavocado.org/content/defense-strategic-planning-rebuttal.

Phase 2
Clarify Mission, Vision, and Values

Having created the plan to plan, it is time to take the first substantive step in the strategic planning process: crafting foundational documents of mission, vision, and perhaps values statements. If they are well articulated, they will not only chart a course for the future but also provide a reference point for revising the plan in response to changing circumstances inside and outside the museum. The museum's specific programs and services, as well as the community and the environment around it, may change, but the mission will remain.

There's no question that developing mission and vision statements requires a significant amount of time and energy, but the return on this investment is significant. The work detailed in this chapter is designed to gather the Strategic Planning Team's collective wisdom on the elements that should be included in the mission, vision, and values statements and to help a task force charged with drafting these foundational documents. As the strategic planning process continues with the environmental scan, feedback from external stakeholders will be incorporated in the team's thinking.

THE CONTEXT OF INSTITUTIONAL HISTORY

Understanding where the museum has been in the past can make it easier to figure out where it is headed in the future, so it is important for the Strategic Planning Team to develop a shared understanding of how the museum came to be what it is today. A good way to do this is to create a timeline that marks key events—milestones, achievements, and setbacks in the history of the institution. Such a chronology may already exist. If not, a staff member, board member, or volunteer could do some research and create one. They might start with annual reports, which usually include the highlights of each year, and publications from anniversary celebrations, which mark institutional milestones.

Another good approach is to involve Strategic Planning Team members during the first meeting, drawing on their memories to create a timeline, perhaps on a roll of newsprint. Encourage everyone to expand the timeline, adding major events and milestones in the museum and in the community at large. After the meeting, the team may want to leave this timeline in a place where staff members can add their reflections and recollections, perhaps in a different color. Veteran staff members have valuable perspectives on the museum's history, and new staff members bring fresh insights. Incorporating the views of both will bridge the museum's past and future, providing a good preface to the creation of mission and vision statements.

When the timeline is complete, highlight those entries that represent institutional traditions and values the team does not want to lose. Then engage the team in a dialogue about the lessons that can be learned from history:

- What has led to institutional stability and growth in the past?
- What forces have caused instability and decline, and how has the museum weathered those challenges?

- What are the most essential qualities and traditions in the museum's past, and how can they be preserved?
- Are there any past decisions that should be reconsidered in order to move forward?

It can also be helpful to put the museum's history in context. How does its evolution relate to the history of museums in the United States and the rest of the world? Context also includes the community and region, its history, and the growth of other civic institutions. Who were the people responsible for the founding and growth of the museum, and were they involved in the community in other ways?

Museums often include a brief history in their strategic plan or on their website. For example, the first paragraph of a longer history of the Whitney Museum of American Art introduces the museum's founder:

> The Whitney Museum of American Art was borne out of sculptor Gertrude Vanderbilt Whitney's advocacy on behalf of living American artists. At the beginning of the twentieth century, artists with new ideas found it nearly impossible to exhibit or sell their work in the United States. Recognizing the obstacles these artists faced, Mrs. Whitney began purchasing and showing their work, thereby becoming the leading patron of American art from 1907 until her death in 1942.[1]

Similarly, the history of the Brooklyn Children's Museum, "the world's first museum designed expressly for children," recognizes its parent institution and early staff leadership:

> The Brooklyn Institute of Arts and Sciences founded the Museum in 1899 as an alternative to existing museums. BCM revolutionized museum-going with its emphasis on participatory exhibits for children and on an educational philosophy of learning through first-hand experience. Anna Billings Gallup, who became curator in 1903, was the Museum's driving force over 35 years. She challenged the staff to enhance children's understanding of themselves and the world in which they live, and to create an interdisciplinary museum experience at the intersection of arts, sciences and world cultures.[2]

THE FOCUS OF MISSION STATEMENTS

If undertaken with serious intent and disciplined insight, the exercise of mission clarification can be one of the most important steps in the entire strategic planning process. An effective mission statement will help board and staff members determine strategy and provide real guidance for the hard work of institutional management. In the words of Larry Butler, "It helps rule some things in and some things out."[3] It will give shape and focus to operating budgets and performance indicators. Looking at the institution's strengths and accomplishments will also suggest strategic directions for the future.

The 2018 study of nonprofit leadership, *Engine of Impact*, stresses "The Primacy of Mission" in the first chapter: "A focused mission that is encapsulated in a clear and concise statement . . . is the foundation on which nonprofit organizations must build their strategy for achieving impact. A clear mission statement should serve to guide all major decisions that a nonprofit organization makes."[4]

The two templates in this chapter are designed to gather the Strategic Planning Team's collective wisdom on the elements that should be included in the mission and vision statements and to help a task force charged with drafting these foundational documents.

- **Template 4: Mission Statement Worksheet** will help Strategic Planning Team members identify the museum's reason for being, its current and targeted audiences, its impact on them, and the means of accomplishing goals.
- **Template 5: Vision Statement Worksheet** will guide a discussion of what success would look like, answering such questions as the following: How will the lives of community members be changed if the museum accomplishes its mission? How will our community, region, nation, or world be changed?

There is a profound difference between a mission statement that works to build commitment and guide strategy and one that functions merely as a public relations blurb. Before a recent strategic planning process, the mission of one museum said:

> The [City] Art Museum shall collect, preserve, and exhibit significant works of contemporary art, western art, art of the Americas, and other cultures. The collection will reflect the diverse heritage of the region in a welcoming environment, which fosters educational and enjoyable art experiences for members and visitors.

Does this statement sound familiar? Not too many years ago, one could substitute the name of almost any museum, adapt the wording that described the collection, and have a mission statement. "Collect, preserve, exhibit, and interpret" were the traditional ingredients in countless museum mission statements. Though most museums perform these functions, such statements are focused on activities rather than impact, on outputs (what the museum does) rather than outcomes (the difference it makes to the people it serves). The previous statement puts the *how* rather than the *why* front and center.

Thinking strategically often requires shifting paradigms. Understanding the difference between outputs and outcomes leads to a fundamental shift in the museum's mission. Outputs are conceived in internal terms. They are the programs and services the museum presents to its visitors and other constituencies. They are easy to quantify but only tangentially related to mission and vision. Outcomes are conceived in external terms. They are the impact the museum's programs and services have on its visitors, who gain new skills, knowledge, attitudes, and values from their museum experiences. Though harder to quantify, they are integrally related to mission and vision. While the second sentence in the above mission statement referred to visitors, it did little to help board or staff members determine strategy or monitor performance.

Distinguishing between outputs and outcomes requires a fundamental paradigm shift for internal stakeholders, who are used to thinking in terms of what they do rather than the impact of their actions. When team members focus on the museum's activities or services, the facilitator can shift the focus by asking what effect these outputs have on visitors and the community. Broadening the frame to consider the impact on specific communities served, over and above the impact on individuals, introduces the concept of what Mark Moore of Harvard University's John F. Kennedy School of Government calls "public value." To the degree that museums have articulated impact, they have generally described the benefits provided to individual patrons, clients, or stakeholders, rather than the improvement of the common good.[5]

Articulating public value requires identifying and understanding the museum's publics or communities. To be sustainable, museums must serve multiple constituencies or audiences. Some are well established and comfortable visiting the museum—school groups, adults and families with deep experience in museumgoing, collectors and scholars, for example. But for others museums remain inaccessible or unwelcoming. In its 2016 Strategic Plan, the American Alliance of Museums highlighted "diversity, equity, accessibility and inclusion in all aspects of museum structure and programming" as one of three focus areas "vital to the future viability, relevance and sustainability of museums."[6] Many museums have acknowledged the need to be more accessible to underserved communities, including people who have limited prior experience (and therefore comfort) with museums, people with different physical or cognitive needs, and people for whom museums are financially inaccessible. Strategic planning is the best opportunity for reframing the museum as a more inclusive and equitable organization, and that process begins with the mission.

Gail Anderson, author of the forthcoming book *Mission Matters: Relevancy and Museums in the 21st Century*, observed:

How a museum frames its role and ultimately its mission is revealing. If a museum sees its role as ally and contributor to the well-being and health of a community, the lens that guides its work is very different from one that focuses inwardly and toward its own benefit. This highlights the importance of shifting the focus away from the institution as a stand-alone entity and toward the museum as a vital and integral part of the ecosystem of its surroundings—fulfilling a role that is needed by the community, and one that can help make a community stronger.[7]

This emphasis on impact requires museums to think expansively and creatively about how their collections, facilities, and programs are relevant to the current needs of their communities and audiences. Nina Simon, executive director of the Museum of Art and History in Santa Cruz, California, defines relevance this way:

> Something is relevant if it gives you new information, if it adds meaning to your life, if it makes a difference to you. It's not enough for something to be familiar, or connected to something you already know. Relevance leads you somewhere. It brings new value to the table.[8]

To figure out how the museum can have a positive, meaningful impact on the lives of its audience and on the community at large, it is critical to keep this notion of relevance in mind. Museums certainly add meaning to the lives of their visitors, and they can make a difference with constituents and communities. Understanding what that difference might be is central to articulating a vibrant, meaningful mission.

THE STRATEGIC IMPACT OF MISSION STATEMENTS

Gail Anderson stresses the importance of museums answering why they exist and how they make a difference: "This requires thinking broadly and having a clear understanding of the issues of the day, empathy and connections with diverse publics, and an institutional humility that is open and welcoming to a wide range of people and perspectives. At the end of the day, museums are facilitators who create ways for people to come together around meaningful and relevant experiences and ideas that reveal new insights and ideally, trigger some level of change."[9]

Like the lifeblood running through a healthy organism, the mission statement infuses the entire institution with energy and purpose. A well-developed mission statement will give the board and staff a platform for program planning, audience development, assessment, and management. It can serve several purposes.

- *Articulate a shared vision that inspires stakeholders.* There is a reason why mission statements strive to be eloquent: language has the power to galvanize and inspire action. The effectiveness of any human enterprise—especially one that must compete for limited amounts of leisure time and rely heavily on volunteer participation—requires alignment of effort across a broad spectrum of players. Think of the museum's mission as a banner the museum holds aloft for all internal and external stakeholders. It should be clear, compelling, and simple enough that anyone affiliated with the museum—board member, staff member, visitor, donor, or volunteer—can quote and understand it. When combined with supporting documents such as a vision statement, it will provide a shared understanding of the museum's purpose and its vision for the future.
- *Announce a distinctive institutional identity.* Strategic thinking is grounded in recognition of the competitive forces that influence any enterprise—commercial or charitable. A museum's mission statement should articulate how it is distinguished from other leisure-time opportunities. Nonprofit status does not exempt a museum from the need to make clear to its various publics how it differs from other organizations that compete for their time, attention, and dollars. In fact, in defining a museum's niche, a mission statement can be a valuable marketing tool.
- *Serve as a tool for decision-making.* No institution can do everything for everyone. Increasing needs and shrinking resources make this painfully clear. Mission statements have a very practical purpose in establishing the basis

for making difficult choices among competing options. A mission that works is one that helps board and staff members decide which programs, exhibitions, and initiatives to pursue and which to eliminate.

- *Enable the measurement of institutional effectiveness.* How will the museum know whether it is successful? How will it monitor and gauge its effectiveness? These questions are of special concern to boards. But there is no single set of metrics that applies to all museums. The museum can measure categories of data—like the number of museum visits or the revenues from museum admission—but what is the impact on visitors' lives? What contribution is the museum making to the communities it serves? The mission statement holds the keys to the metrics that will answer these questions.

THE BOARD'S ROLE IN ARTICULATING MISSION

As holders of the DNA of institutional mission, vision, and values, board members have a special role to play in shaping the statements that are touchstones for the strategic thinking, planning, and implementation that follow. That role will vary, depending upon the institutional culture, the age and size of the museum, the relationship between the director and the board, and a variety of other factors. At minimum, the board is the impetus for building an institution-wide consensus around mission. If the current mission statement serves all of the purposes outlined above, board members should use it as a guide for all of their actions and decisions, and the director should encourage staff members to do the same. If not, the board is the body to set in motion a process for either revisiting and refreshing the museum's understanding of its mission (which might require minor edits) or creating a brand-new mission.

In describing the shortcomings of many mission statements, Anderson says, "Most museums use an internal approach to identify their role in society. Thus, their mission statements reflect an inward focus rather than an outward-looking stance. By creating a mission process that is externally responsive, each institution has the opportunity to find that unique role that is relevant and makes a difference to its community."[10] Because of their involvement in numerous and varied facets of the community, board members can help to ensure that the mission statement focuses on the needs of diverse individuals and the community at large.

ASSESSING THE CURRENT MISSION STATEMENT

Unless the museum is new, it probably has a mission statement and perhaps other supporting documents. Standards for mission statements have evolved over the years; however, many are still overly long and focused on the museums' activities. Language that seemed appropriate ten years ago may now feel hackneyed or dated. If the existing mission is not widely embraced by board and staff members, it will not be used to describe the museum's reasons for being or to inform decision-making.

William F. Meehan III and Kim Starkey Jonker advise that a well-crafted mission statement should act as a "lodestar," keeping an organization on course. In assessing a mission, they note that "a well-conceived mission statement . . . can guide an organization in making key decisions." It should:

1. Be focused
2. Solve unmet public needs
3. Leverage distinctive skills
4. Guide trade-offs
5. Inspire and be inspired by key stakeholders
6. Be timeless
7. Be sticky[11]

To begin the strategic planning process with a review of the mission, distribute copies of the current statement and any supporting documents at an early meeting of the Strategic Planning Team. Write the entire mission statement on a large flip chart (or charts, depending on the length). Set out green and red markers and invite team members to come to the flip chart and share their reflections.

- Underline in green the words and phrases that resonate for them, in light of previous discussions about **Report 3: Strategic Planning Team Responses**, and write new words and phrases where they fit in.
- Use red lines to strike out words and phrases that are not essential or useful in the ways described above and put question marks by sections that are unclear.

When everyone has had an opportunity to participate, bring the entire team to the flip chart and engage in a dialogue about places where there are many underlines or strikethroughs. Be sure to consider suggestions of new words and outlier responses as well, asking for clarification if necessary. Are there any sections that are questionable, ambiguous, or unclear?

Having considered individual words and phrases, ask these more general questions:

- Is this mission useful as a decision-making tool? Does it help board and staff members allocate their time and resources?
- Is it clear and simple enough that anyone affiliated with the museum can remember and repeat it, at least in principle?
- Does it show a sense of connectedness to the museum's communities, the greater world, and the issues of our times?
- Is it inspirational? Does it impel trustees, staff members, and volunteers to work toward a common cause?
- Does it distinguish the museum from other similar institutions?
- Does it identify the parameters or focus of the collection and the reasons for them?
- Does it clearly identify the current audience as well as segments of the community that need to be better served?
- Is it measurable? Without articulating specific metrics, the mission statement should suggest ways to demonstrate success.

After engaging in a dialogue based on these questions, the team will be in a position to reach consensus on whether the mission statement needs to be rewritten or whether relatively minor edits will correct deficiencies. Ask for a show of hands for agreement or disagreement with the statement "Our current museum statement continues to serve as a touchstone for our work." If there is consensus on the need for a new mission, it's better to start with a clean slate than to try to revise the old one.

CRAFTING A NEW MISSION STATEMENT

The work of writing a new mission statement begins with a set of questions designed to elicit ideas and then moves to using **Template 4: Mission Statement Worksheet** to organize key words, phrases, and concepts. A small task force will weave these elements together in a draft, which will be presented to the entire team and revised, as needed.

To set the tone for creating a mission that is transformative and inspirational, the Strategic Planning Team should first engage in some "blue-sky thinking" about the future of the museum. This is the time to elicit big ideas, hopes, and dreams for the museum and the communities it serves. There will be plenty of opportunities for logical thinking and quantitative measurements later in the process.

TEMPLATE 4: MISSION STATEMENT WORKSHEET

Guiding Questions	Responses That Resonate
Purpose Why does the museum exist?	
Community Who does the museum serve or seek to serve?	
Impact What impacts do we want to have on our visitors and our communities?	
Methods How do we use our resources to serve our communities?	

When the team is ready to give words to its dreams for the museum, consider four elements found in many effective mission statements: purpose, community, impact, and methods. Again, **Report 3: Strategic Planning Team Responses** may provide a good starting point, especially the responses to the question about community and purpose. Consider the following questions about each element, making notes on four separate flip charts:

Purpose

- Why does the museum exist? What need or needs must we serve?
- What makes our museum uniquely valuable?
- What is the passion that drives us forward?
- If presented with the resources that the museum has today without any assumptions about what a museum is supposed to be, what purpose would we choose?

Community

- On whose behalf do we exist?
- Draw a diagram of the various communities within our community.
- What communities do we currently serve?
- What new communities must we serve in order to increase our public value?

Impact

- What impact do our programs and services have on various communities and audiences?
- How will their lives be changed as a result of visiting the museum or participating in our programs?
- What outcomes are most valuable to the communities identified above?
- What are the greatest needs in the community at large, and how could the museum have a positive impact?

Methods

- What will be most effective in fulfilling our purposes and creating valuable outcomes for our communities?
- What are the most valuable programs and services we currently provide, from the perspectives of the communities we serve?
- What new programs and services do our communities need or want?

As respondents answer the questions about the museum's purpose, community, impact, and methods, the administrator will record all responses. It isn't necessary to think in terms of complete sentences at this early stage of the mission-making process. Words, phrases, and concepts are what matter most. Wordsmithing will come later.

A small task force that includes skillful writers and sharp-eyed editors can take this work to the next stage, using the administrator's notes and **Template 4: Mission Statement Worksheet**. Task force members will first review the notes independently, selecting the words and phrases they find most cogent and powerful, then come together as a group to incorporate the language they selected in Template 4. Begin the conversation with a dialogue about why each person selected the phrases they did, and then build consensus around which phrases are most essential. Those that emerge in each area (purpose, community, impact, and methods) can be assembled in a variety of ways.

Many mission statements shy away from commitment to outcomes, hedging their bets with words like *seek* or *intend*. However, the mission of any organization is not to *try* to accomplish its goals but to actually *succeed*! A mission statement is a place to be bold, inspiring commitment and leading to results.

After experimenting with different ways of weaving the four aspects of mission together, create one or more draft statements and circulate them to the entire Strategic Planning Team. Put a review of the draft(s) on the agenda at the next meeting and allow plenty of time for dialogue. Incorporate team members' suggestions in a revised draft and circulate it again. It may require several revisions to arrive at a mission statement the entire team supports, but once there is agreement, present it to the board for approval, explaining the Strategic Planning Team's thought process and the steps that led to consensus. Be sure to acknowledge the contributions of the entire team and the task force members and thank them publicly.

Even with a shared sense of satisfaction among Strategic Planning Team members and the board's approval of the mission, it is sometimes better to put off finalizing the draft until later in the planning process. As planning progresses, team members may develop a clearer understanding of exactly how the mission is shaping their thinking and decision-making, enabling them to articulate the mission more clearly.

MANY APPROACHES TO MISSION

There are many approaches that can be taken to articulating an institution's mission. There are several sample statements, from a variety of museums, in the appendix.

Kevin Starr, director of the Mulago Foundation, argues for extreme brevity:

A verb, a target population, and an outcome that implies something to measure—and we want it in eight words or less. Why eight words? It just seems to work. It's long enough to be specific and short enough to force clarity. Save kids' lives in Uganda. Rehabilitate coral reefs in the Western Pacific. Prevent maternal-child transmission of HIV in Africa. Get Zambian farmers out of poverty. These statements tell us exactly what the organization has set out to accomplish.[12]

Few museums aim for such brevity, but many mission statements would benefit from tighter editing and focus. Starr's examples do not include any *methods* by which these agencies achieve their goals—a notable omission. However, several are crystal clear about *audiences*, which is a shortcoming of many museum mission statements.

Ultimately, compelling mission statements have more in common with poetry than business communication. They use active, evocative language rather than jargon. They are short and direct rather than lengthy and convoluted. The examples in the appendix are inspiring and poetic, and they capture the distinctive nature of the institutions.[13] Some include the methods they use to achieve their missions, but in others the means are not spelled out. In general, the intended audiences are quite vague in many museum mission statements.

VISION STATEMENTS

If a mission statement provides a blueprint for the museum's work, a vision statement is an artist's rendering of the institution at some point in the future. It articulates what successful achievement of the mission looks like. It is a depiction that everyone can visualize and embrace, like Martin Luther King's "I have a dream" or John F. Kennedy's commitment to land a man on the moon before the end of the 1960s.[14]

A vision should be bold, compelling, and motivating; it should not be constrained by current limitations or available resources. The idea is to define a desired set of possibilities for the future. One board consultant observed that "a vision is guided by dreams, not constraints."[15]

The picture created by the vision has two perspectives—external and internal. To paint the external perspective, consider the following questions:

- Who are our stakeholders, and how will they interact with the museum?
- What mix of programs and services will attract, serve, and sustain them?

- How will the lives of community members be changed if the museum accomplishes its mission?
- How will our community, region, nation, or world be changed?

To envision the internal perspective, consider the following questions:

- How will the museum need to change in order to achieve our mission?
- How will trustees, staff members, and volunteers interact with one another and with our audiences?
- What facilities, technologies, and funding sources will be needed to support our mission?

A vision statement is a picture of the institution operating effectively to realize its mission. To stimulate the kind of thinking that will shape this vision, ask members of the Strategic Planning Team to engage in a short writing exercise, individually or in small groups. Imagine it is the same date, five years in the future, or at a significant celebration, such as an anniversary or other milestone. The local newspaper has just run an article about the museum's new initiatives, its impact on the community, and its board and staff leadership. What does the headline say? How does the first paragraph read? What are the main points?

To arrive at a shared vision, look for the common elements in the responses, and assign a task force responsibility for building a draft vision statement on those themes. This may be the same group that drafted the mission statement or a new group. Use the same techniques as in writing the mission statement—gathering input, coming to consensus, writing a draft to circulate to the entire Strategic Planning Team, and incorporating comments in a final version. **Template 5: Vision Statement Worksheet** is used the same way as **Template 4: Mission Statement Worksheet**.

THE VARIOUS DIMENSIONS OF VISION

Reviewing museum vision statements also reveals a wide range of approaches. Some are focused on the change the museum effects in the community or on a broader scale. Other statements position the museum as a leader in its field or region. Still others, particularly those of publicly funded museums, articulate impact in terms of economic drivers or numbers of people (often schoolchildren) served. Some museums have switched to calling these "impact" statements or, to distinguish them from financial impact, "social impact" statements.

As with mission statements, vision statements that aim for social impact are generally more powerful drivers of organizational effectiveness. While excellence and leadership are laudable goals, they are ultimately inward, self-referential visions. Consider, for example, these vision statements:

The [city] Museum is recognized as a leading center for scholarship, engagement, and investigation of [state] and [region].

Our vision is to be [the state's] leading statewide collecting institution and learning center for social, family, and cultural history.

The [name] Museum will be recognized for its imaginative programming and as a sought-after resource for study, knowledge, and engagement by local and national audiences.

The [name] will be known as a global leader among museums.

While one could argue that these museums would not achieve recognition or stature as leaders without providing services of value, ultimately these visions are about their reputation, not their impact on the communities they serve.

TEMPLATE 5: VISION STATEMENT WORKSHEET

Guiding Questions	Responses That Resonate
Headline	
Lead sentence or paragraph	
Community impact	
Staff, board, other internal impact	
Sustainability	
Other	

For some particularly effective vision statements, paired with mission statements from the same museums, please see the appendix.

VALUES STATEMENTS

Mission and vision statements are, by definition, brief and succinct. Sometimes they alone cannot convey the full range of ideas that drive a museum and the impacts they inspire. Some museums support and amplify their mission and vision statements by articulating institutional values, core beliefs, or guiding principles. Values statements answer the question: What are the fundamental values and beliefs that guide the museum's interactions with its external and internal stakeholders? They identify the guiding tenets of daily life in the museum, defining the underlying beliefs and suggesting standards of behavior.

Too often values statements are long lists of lofty ambitions without a clear sense of their implications for specific organizations. Living out institutional values requires commitment of resources, as well as recognition of the fact that values often exist in tension—for example, accessibility and preservation. Innovation, which often appears on values statements, is laudable and exciting; however, it can also be risky and expensive.

The Strategic Planning Team might begin by discussing how the museum would use a values statement and reviewing examples from other institutions. There are several creative and inspiring examples in the appendix. If the team decides to draft a values statement, a task force can initiate conversations about values, draft a statement, and circulate drafts to the entire team for their feedback.

Because values statements should capture the unique culture of the museum, the input of staff members and volunteers is critical to a statement that accurately reflects the entire institution and inspires the support of internal stakeholders. The task force might meet with staff and volunteer representatives or invite input in other ways. One creative approach is to post leading questions such as "What do we value as an organization?" or "What makes this museum special?" in a common area, like a break room or near the copy machine, and invite comments, providing markers and sticky notes.

Mission, vision, and values statements are at the heart of strategic thinking and planning. Articulating the museum's aspirations and core beliefs at the outset of this process provides a framework and firm foundation for the decision-making and priority setting to come.

NOTES

1. Whitney Museum of American Art, "History of the Whitney," accessed January 22, 2018, https://whitney.org/About/History.

2. Brooklyn Children's Museum, "History: The World's First Children's Museum," accessed January 22, 2018, https://www.brooklynkids.org/about/history/.

3. Email from Larry Butler, March 20, 2018.

4. William F. Meehan III and Kim Starkey Jonker, *Engine of Impact* (Stanford, CA: Stanford University Press, 2018), 27.

5. Mark H. Moore, *Creating Public Value* (Cambridge, MA: Harvard University Press, 1997).

6. American Alliance of Museums, "2016–2020 Strategic Plan," accessed January 22, 2018, https://www.aam-us.org/programs/about-aam/american-alliance-of-museums-strategic-plan/.

7. Gail Anderson, interview with the authors, February 25, 2018.

8. Nina Simon, *The Art of Relevance* (Santa Cruz, CA: Museum 2.0, 2016), 29.

9. Anderson interview.

10. Ibid.

11. Meehan and Jonker, *Engine of Impact*, 29–30.

12. Kevin Starr, "The Eight Word Mission Statement," *Stanford Social Innovation Review*, September 18, 2012, accessed January 18, 2018, https://ssir.org/articles/entry/the_eight_word_mission_statement.

13. The authors acknowledge the excellent research of Gail Anderson, who contributed several of these examples.

14. Michael Allison and Jude Kaye, *Strategic Planning for Nonprofit Organizations: A Practical Guide and Workbook* (New York: John Wiley & Sons, 1997), 68.

15. Kay Sprinkel Grace, *The Nonprofit Board's Role in Strategic Planning* (Washington, DC: National Center for Nonprofit Boards, 1996), 14.

3

Phase 3

Scan the Environment

Having looked inward to articulate the mission, vision, and values, it is now time to look outward into the communities the museum serves. The Strategic Planning Team will need to not only enhance its understanding of audiences the museum currently serves but also consider broader perspectives. External stakeholders include museum members and visitors, teachers, students, and school district administrators, as well as experts in the museum's discipline, community organizations, current and potential partners, and funders. Thinking strategically requires considering all possible perspectives and determining which could have the greatest impact on the museum's future.

The environmental scan encourages a review of all the major external forces that have an influence on the institution. This phase (sometimes called a "situational analysis") will require very active participation by internal and external stakeholders on the Strategic Planning Team: board and staff members and other constituents. But it is time well spent because this phase lays the groundwork for the next, which is to identify and prioritize the strategic issues the museum must address in order to move forward and realize its mission. Good information at this stage will lead to good decisions later.

The three templates in this chapter will help the team collect and record critical issues, identify additional information needs, and develop a plan to scan the environment.

- **Template 6: Critical Issues Inventory** is a place to keep track of all the issues that emerge during the Strategic Planning Team's discussions, recording how and when each issue surfaces and identifying needs for additional information.
- **Template 7: Information-Gathering Plan** will help the Strategic Planning Team create a database of concrete information. Starting with the questions raised in Template 6, the team can identify needed perspectives, choose data-gathering methods, and assign responsibilities to team, board, and staff members.
- **Template 8: Information-Gathering Summary** will ensure that the research results are collected in a consistent and comprehensive way so the Strategic Planning Team can build on them in identifying strategic initiatives.

KEEPING TRACK OF CRITICAL ISSUES

Critical issues will emerge from a variety of sources: review of background information about the museum, reflection on **Report 3: Strategic Planning Team Responses**, discussion of the institutional timeline, development of mission and vision statements, and conversations with stakeholders. These issues will be refined as additional information is gathered, and new issues will arise throughout the planning process, but often the first issues to be identified are of considerable strategic import.

Template 6: Critical Issues Inventory is a running list of issues the team wants to keep track of as it moves through the process. Planners might think of it as a "parking lot" for ideas. In a sense, this template fuels the strategic thinking and planning that follows. It also provides an important historical record of the evolution of the Strategic Planning Team's thinking because it captures not only the issues but also their sources and the questions they raise.

TEMPLATE 6: CRITICAL ISSUES INVENTORY

Critical Issue	Source	Questions Related to This Issue

In the first column, list the needs and challenges that surface in early meetings of the Strategic Planning Team, adding to this list throughout the process. Knowing the source of an issue can be important as the team continues to refine and explore it. To keep track of where issues originated, list sources in the second column (for example, "Strategic Planning Team Survey" or "discussion with mayor"). In the third column, list information needed and unanswered questions raised about each issue. At this point the issues are simply collected and recorded. They will be prioritized in **Template 7: Information-Gathering Plan**.

Before moving on, look at the issues listed in column 1 to see what they have in common. Observing connections is an aspect of strategic thinking that will come into play throughout the planning process. Are there issues that are connected, such as challenges related to financial stability or community-wide needs that suggest forming partnerships with other institutions? If so, start to cluster these issues.

GATHERING THE INFORMATION NEEDED TO PLAN

The Strategic Planning Team needs a plan to coordinate the efforts of the many internal and external stakeholders who will be involved in conducting the environmental scan. **Template 7: Information-Gathering Plan** will help design a detailed study to be conducted by team members with support from staff, board, and community members.

- In column 1, *Critical Issue*, summarize no more than ten core issues from **Template 6: Critical Issues Inventory**. At this stage, it may help to phrase each issue as a question. For example, *improve visibility* becomes *How can we raise the museum's profile in the community?*
- In column 2, *Questions to Be Answered*, list any additional information needed to think strategically about each issue. Sort and cluster the questions from column 3 of Template 6, looking for connections with critical issues in column 1 and rephrasing them to be as specific as possible. For example: *Where might we forge mutually beneficial partnerships to make the museum more relevant to the African American community?*
- In column 3, *Perspectives to Seek*, list the names of individuals and organizations that can provide the information needed to answer each question. If the Strategic Planning Team includes a diverse set of stakeholders, they will have access to many contacts in the wider community. Museum staff members and volunteers, as well as colleagues at partner institutions and civic offices, might also be able to suggest contacts.
- Identify appropriate techniques for gathering information about each critical issue, and list them in column 4, *Methodology*. In addition to formal methods such as community meetings, focus groups, questionnaires, online surveys, and exit interviews, consider informal methods such as one-on-one conversations, visits to other museums and related institutions, and anecdotal information. Also consider information that might already be available in the museum, such as visitor studies, project evaluations, financial records, and attendance records. External sources of information in the community, region, or state might include departments of education, travel and tourism offices, economic development agencies, and demographers. Online resources include other museums' websites with their annual reports and strategic plans, websites that analyze census or other data sets, and state and federal cultural agencies. Also consider what might be available through professional organizations such as state, regional, and national museum associations.
- In column 5, *Responsibility*, identify individuals or small groups who will be responsible for information gathering. Try to involve all members of the Strategic Planning Team, aiming for relatively even distribution of responsibility so that no one is overburdened and everyone has a chance to participate actively in this critical stage of the planning process. In helping to collect data, team members are also building valuable connections in the community. Don't hesitate to reach beyond the Strategic Planning Team to include staff members and volunteers, who often appreciate the opportunity to have a stake in the planning process.

TEMPLATE 7: INFORMATION-GATHERING PLAN

Critical Issue	Questions to Be Answered	Perspectives to Seek	Methodology	Responsibility	Time Frame

- In column 6, *Time Frame*, indicate the time frame for gathering the necessary information. In choosing the methodology and making assignments, consider how much time is available, given the length of the planning process and meeting schedule. A large group of information gatherers with discrete, manageable assignments will shorten the overall time frame.

CHOOSING THE APPROPRIATE RESEARCH STRATEGY

With so many ways to gather information from community members and constituents, it makes sense to choose the most efficient and effective. The general guideline about market research is that more individualized techniques are used with the most critical or significant sources of information, and more general strategies with larger groups of informants. For example, one might productively conduct an online survey with all of the fourth-grade teachers in a community and schedule a one-on-one interview with the superintendent of schools. The team should make it easy and convenient for the people who are being asked to contribute their ideas and expertise. For example, rather than expecting community partners to come to the museum, team members should plan on visiting them at their sites, which not only makes it more convenient for respondents but also gives the team a sense of their operations and programs. Take advantage of regularly scheduled meetings. For example, if there is a regular training session for museum docents, request some time on the agenda to ask questions relevant to planning.

Case in point: A relatively new director used the environmental scan to cement relationships with many individuals and groups with which the museum had ongoing relationships as well as potential partners. In the course of the planning process, she sat down with more than thirty individuals across the state. While it was time consuming to travel to their offices, she found that showing respect for her partners' time and expertise paid off.

The intent of the environmental scan is to learn more about issues and trends in the community, best practices and successful initiatives at other institutions, and challenges they face. For interviews, focus groups, or community meetings, develop a short and focused list of open-ended questions. Start by asking informants for their insights and observations. If they are in a position to explain the work of their community agency or organization, ask about their plans and priorities. Keep the focus on the informant and their organization, not the museum, for at least the first half of the allotted time. In the second half of the meeting, interviewers might ask about their experience or impressions of the museum and their thoughts about how the museum might begin to address some of the critical issues that have been identified. Structuring conversations this way accomplishes several things. First, it honors and reinforces the expertise of the people being interviewed. Second, it makes it more comfortable to engage others in conversations about the museum's future. Third, it invites informants to play a vital role in the planning process. And if they are interested in how the process unfolds, offer to send them a copy of the final plan.

APPLYING THE FINDINGS

Ask those responsible for gathering information to summarize what they learned using **Template 8: Information-Gathering Summary** so that the planning team has a record of the findings. Team members will complete a separate sheet for each interview, summarizing the feedback they gathered in a clear and concise way and noting which of the questions were relevant to that interview. Each team member should then summarize the most important insights in preparation for the next meeting of the Strategic Planning Team. The goal is to give other team members what they need to know to make decisions, not to impress them with how much information was collected.

Share these written reports in advance of the next meeting of the Strategic Planning Team so members can begin to digest the feedback. Those who gathered information will report briefly on their findings at the meeting, highlighting the single most surprising or significant bit of information they gathered and answering any questions. The administrator or person serving as facilitator should summarize the key findings on flip charts or a white board and

TEMPLATE 8: INFORMATION-GATHERING SUMMARY

Name of interviewer:

Name of interviewee:

Affiliation and/or position:

Date of interview:

Possible questions to be answered (from Template 7):

☐

☐

☐

☐

☐

☐

Please check which of the preceding questions the interview covered and summarize responses to each.

Key points from the interview:

Most surprising comment:

Team member's highlights and main takeaways:

share these with the team after the meeting. When aggregated, the data will show how the museum is perceived by particular stakeholders and by the community at large. After looking at key findings, the team should be challenged to describe the picture that has been painted of the museum's current operating environment.

Case in point: One museum used an online survey tool in an innovative way, not to collect feedback but to record the results of interviews. The Strategic Planning Team developed a list of stakeholders to interview and six questions, which were incorporated in an online survey. Each team member was assigned two people on the list. While they were conducting the interviews, they took notes, and then they logged into the survey tool to enter responses for each interview they conducted. There were several advantages to this approach: the work was parceled out into manageable pieces, all of the findings were recorded in a single place, and no one had to decipher handwriting! Four years later, when the organization was once again engaged in planning, it was easy to copy the questions, repeat the process, and compare the results.

With the clearer picture of the museum's present state that is provided by the environmental scan, the Strategic Planning Team is in a position to ask questions that will help it think strategically about the future:

- What threads are woven throughout the reports, and what trends do they suggest?
- What have we learned about the communities within our community and their specific priorities?
- What community resources might be interested in collaborative initiatives?
- What current services and programs do our communities value most?
- What other services and programs do they need?
- Where might we find financial and in-kind support for these new programs?
- What other activities compete for the time of our communities, and how can we attract their interest and participation?
- What other organizations aim to serve these same communities? Is there potential to collaborate rather than compete?
- Who are our greatest potential allies?
- What positive perceptions can we build on?
- What negative perceptions must we overcome?

Case in point: An art museum began planning with a sense that it needed to become essential to its community, which was an economically challenged city, but without a concrete idea of what that meant. The first community meeting included civic leaders: the mayor, state representative, chief of police, fire chief, head of economic development, superintendent of schools, vice president of the local state college, and staff and board members from the public library and historical society. Participants talked about community needs and the plans of other organizations in the city. One of the themes that emerged was "we need you to bet on this city's future." The feedback shaped the museum's exhibition, education, marketing, and facilities plans. It is now widely cited as an example of a civically engaged museum and was recognized by the state arts council.

EXPANDING THE SCOPE OF THE ENVIRONMENTAL SCAN

The answers to the Strategic Planning Team's initial questions often generate new questions. When the environmental scan reveals the need for additional information, it may lead to such specific questions as:

- Do we need to do a more in-depth analysis of our audiences? Do our surveys call for larger sample sizes?
- Do we need to learn more about the resources or reputation of a potential partner?

- Would a site visit to another museum or cultural organization in the area help us position ourselves more strategically?
- Do we have the resources needed to consider adding a new program or service? What funds are available from local sources? What regional and national grant opportunities are available?
- Do we need a sharper understanding of the performance of the museum's endowment, income projections, or visitation patterns?

It will require patience on the part of the Strategic Planning Team to postpone decision-making and to invest additional time and energy in gathering more information if needed. But each time board and staff members go out into the community, there is potential to forge stronger connections that will be useful in implementing the strategic plan. Getting to know the community's needs has a long-term benefit that can extend beyond the life of the strategic plan. It creates a more knowledgeable and responsive board, a wider sphere of engagement and influence, and a strengthened institution.

4

Phase 4

Determine Strategies

While each phase of the strategic planning process is critical to the next, this phase is arguably the most pivotal. The seven phases of strategic planning flow from one to another (see figure 0.14, p. xxiv), with Phase 4 at the heart of the process. The first three phases lead directly into it, and the last three proceed from it. It is, in more than a figurative sense, the hub of the strategic planning wheel.

This phase represents a turning point from divergent to convergent thinking (see figure 0.15, p. xxv). Up to this point, the Strategic Planning Team, the board, and the staff have been engaged in a series of individual and group activities designed to gather information from a variety of sources, tapping into their collective memory and increasing their evolving understanding of the current perspectives and insights of multiple stakeholders. At this stage the team must make a critical transition to convergent thinking in an effort to bring together all of the feedback gathered in the environmental scan and reach consensus about how to respond to the critical issues that are of greatest strategic import. As it begins to develop strategies, it will also shift from the hand wringing that can come with recognizing the challenges the institution faces to the head scratching that is needed to identify potential solutions. Now the Strategic Planning Team will begin the very challenging and rewarding work that is the essence of strategic thinking: making choices from the many available and often competing options.

This phase also marks the midpoint in the process. All the hard work and creative thinking that have been done to date have laid a strong foundation on which to build specific strategies. To make the most of the efforts of internal and external stakeholders, the Strategic Planning Team should follow two creative thinking exercises described in this chapter step by step. The first, framed by **Template 9: SWOT Matrix**, analyzes the strengths, weaknesses, opportunities, and threats in the institution and the environment. The second, shaped by **Template 10: Strategic Priorities Quadrant**, identifies the issues that are most important now. These exercises will shift from divergent thinking and set the wheels of convergent thinking in motion. The processes are mutually informative. By relating them, considering the implications of both, and seeking connections between them, the team's thinking will move from the "what?" to the "so what?"

The Strategic Planning Team will emerge from this phase with a clear set of strategic initiatives, long-range goals, and concrete, measurable objectives. The increasing clarity around mission and vision will help the team prioritize the critical issues and determine how the museum will best deploy its limited resources—human, physical, and financial—over the next three to five years. At this point, critical issues become strategic initiatives. This important work is accomplished with the help of three templates:

- **Template 9: SWOT Matrix** analyzes strengths, weaknesses, opportunities, and threats to suggest strategic initiatives.

- **Template 10: Strategic Priorities Quadrant** helps identify the most urgent and significant issues.
- **Template 11A: Strategic Initiatives Worksheet** and **Template 11B: Goals and Objectives Worksheet** draw together the results of Templates 9 and 10 to identify strategic initiatives, goals, and objectives and assign responsibilities and time frames for each.

USING THE INFORMATION GATHERED IN THE ENVIRONMENTAL SCAN

The variety of information gathered in the environmental scan can be organized in many ways, according to positive and negative factors, knowns and unknowns, short-term and long-term issues, and degree of risk. One familiar system is to identify the strengths, weaknesses, opportunities, and threats (SWOTs) and organize them into a SWOT Matrix. Begin by asking the following questions:

- What are our strengths? What advantages do we have over other institutions and experiences competing for our communities' limited amounts of leisure time?
- What are our weaknesses—both in a tactical sense and more systemically?
- What opportunities exist in the community and in the operating environment?
- What situations or trends pose threats to our sustainability or impediments to our success?

As team members explore the answers to these questions, they will discover that strengths and weaknesses usually turn out to be internal to the organization, while opportunities and threats are generally external.

Template 9: SWOT Matrix has four sections to be filled in by the Strategic Planning Team (or broader groups of board and staff members if more input is needed). Working together or in small groups, stakeholders will list strengths in the upper-left quadrant, weaknesses in the upper right, opportunities in the lower left, and threats in the lower right.

Figure 4.1 shows the SWOTs identified by the Strategic Planning Team of a university natural history museum. Seeing the strengths opposite the weaknesses makes it possible to observe which weaknesses are the flip sides of strengths. For example, a great historic facility has architectural charm, community history, and memories associated with it. But along with these strengths come outdated mechanical systems that compromise collections care and limit visitor access and amenities. The SWOT grid format also shows how threats can suggest related opportunities. For example, concern about competition from nearby science museums can lead to new opportunities if it inspires the museum to become clearer about its mission, more articulate in carving out a niche for itself, and more creative in exploring possible collaborations with neighboring museums.

TEMPLATE 9: SWOT MATRIX

Identify SWOTs

Insert words or phrases into the matrix below describing the museum's strengths, weaknesses, opportunities, and threats.

Strengths		Weaknesses	
S1		W1	
S2		W2	
S3		W3	
S4		W4	
S5		W5	
S6		W6	
S7		W7	
S8		W8	
S9		W9	
S10		W10	
Opportunities		**Threats**	
O1		T1	
O2		T2	
O3		T3	
O4		T4	
O5		T5	
O6		T6	
O7		T7	
O8		T8	
O9		T9	
O10		T10	

Strengths			Weaknesses	
S1	Amazing artifacts and specimens	W1	Small staff
S2	Great historic facility	W2	Limited financial resources
S3	Credibility, resources of University	W3	Lack of cohesive interpretation
S4	Student docent program	W4	Limited parking
S5	Academic appeal interdisciplinary programs	W5	Outdated exhibits
S6	Location on central campus	W6	Weak relations w/ academic departments
S7	Fiscal responsibility	W7	Outdated facilities
S8	Relationships w/ other University museums	W8	Lack of reputation
Opportunities			**Threats**	
O1	Play a role in student, faculty recruitment	T1	Lack of awareness
O2	Collaboration using new Planetarium	T2	University funding cuts
O3	Draw on large population base	T3	Public school funding cuts
O4	Collaborate w/ nearby science museums	T4	New location off central campus
O5	Funding for research dissemination	T5	Competition from nearby museums
O6	New building w/ state of the art facilities	T6	Soft money not sustainable
O7	Better define niche	T7	Local economy tied to world events
O8	Private & corporate regional funding base	T8	Priorities of new University administration

FIGURE 4.1
SWOT Example (Courtesy of the Museum Trustee Association)

Once each quadrant has been completed, a small group of Strategic Planning Team members can draw lines connecting strengths with weaknesses and opportunities with threats. Alternatively, they can re-sort the lists thematically to show alignment. After exploring the relationships, all team members can use dot voting (see "Take Note!" on p. 59) or some other means of prioritizing the greatest strengths and the most serious weaknesses, as well as the biggest opportunities and threats to come to consensus on the SWOTs that are most critical to the future of the institution. Zeroing in on three to five issues in each category will help the Strategic Planning Team decide where to focus its attention in developing the plan. This is a case in which less is more: more than five strategic issues are likely to become unwieldy and unlikely to be achieved. The prioritized strengths, weaknesses, opportunities, and threats will be used in the next exercise.

SWOTS AS THE BASIS FOR STRATEGIC THINKING

The SWOT Matrix not only helps in identifying and organizing the museum's specific strengths, weaknesses, opportunities, and threats but also can help in crafting strategies for building on strengths, overcoming weaknesses, utilizing opportunities, and minimizing threats. Here is where this strategic planning approach breaks new ground in the use of the familiar SWOT paradigm. By applying four different types of thinking to the internal strengths and weaknesses and the external opportunities and threats, the Strategic Planning Team can begin to identify "operations" or courses of action that will evolve into strategic initiatives, goals, or objectives.

Applicative thinking considers how to directly apply strengths to overcome weaknesses and diminish threats. The arrows in figure 4.2 suggest the direction of the Strategic Planning Team's thought process. An example of a strength that can be applied to diminish a threat is: *The museum's strong sense of fiscal responsibility and proactive budgeting procedures can help moderate fluctuations in endowment revenue.*

Transformative thinking seeks to transform weaknesses into strengths and threats into opportunities. The arrows in figure 4.3 suggest the direction of the Strategic Planning Team's thought process. An example of a weakness that can be transformed into a strength is: *The lack of cohesive interpretive thrust in current exhibits leaves room for a completely new vision of the visitor experience.*

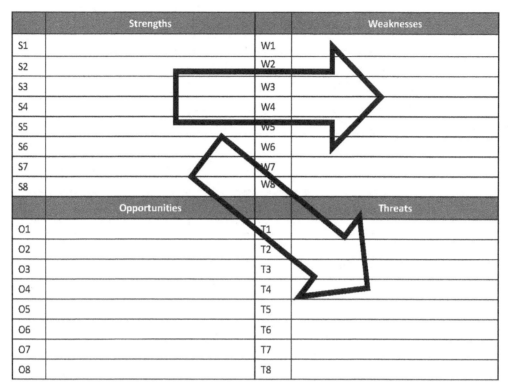

FIGURE 4.2
Applicative Thinking (Courtesy of the Museum Trustee Association)

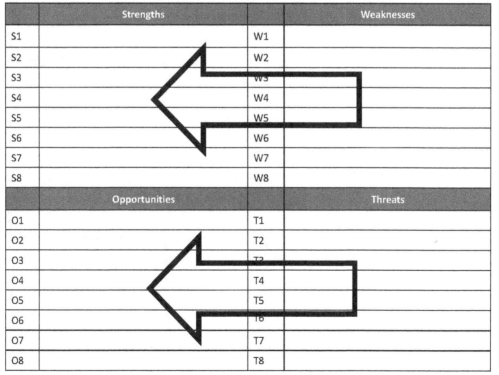

FIGURE 4.3
Transformative Thinking (Courtesy of the Museum Trustee Association)

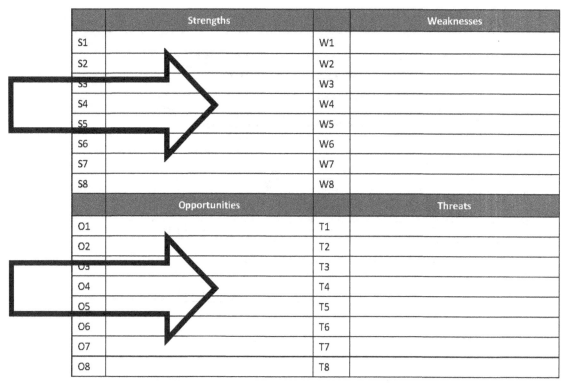

	Strengths		Weaknesses
S1		W1	
S2		W2	
S3		W3	
S4		W4	
S5		W5	
S6		W6	
S7		W7	
S8		W8	
	Opportunities		Threats
O1		T1	
O2		T2	
O3		T3	
O4		T4	
O5		T5	
O6		T6	
O7		T7	
O8		T8	

FIGURE 4.4
Additive Thinking (Courtesy of the Museum Trustee Association)

	Strengths		Weaknesses
S1		W1	
S2		W2	
S3		W3	
S4		W4	
S5		W5	
S6		W6	
S7		W7	
S8		W8	
	Opportunities		Threats
O1		T1	
O2		T2	
O3		T3	
O4		T4	
O5		T5	
O6		T6	
O7		T7	
O8		T8	

FIGURE 4.5
Subtractive Thinking (Courtesy of the Museum Trustee Association)

Additive thinking considers how to add new strengths and opportunities to those the museum already has. The arrows in figure 4.4 suggest how this type of thinking will bring new ideas about strengths and opportunities into the picture. An example of an opportunity that can be added to current programming is: *Increase the museum's impact on the community by developing outreach programs with support from the community foundation.*

Subtractive thinking seeks to diminish or eliminate weaknesses and threats that characterize or confront the institution. The arrows in figure 4.5 suggest moving weaknesses and threats out of the picture. An example of a weakness that can be diminished is: *Assess the impact of current programs to determine which can be reduced or eliminated in order to lighten the workload and free staff to develop new initiatives.*

Put this exercise on the agenda for a Strategic Planning Team meeting. If time permits, the entire team can work together to develop ideas for all four operations. If time is short, break up into small groups or "strategic think tanks." If there are four groups, each one can work on one type of thinking. If there are two, one group can work on applicative and transformative thinking while the other works on additive and subtractive. Ask each group to prioritize the operations they generate, presenting their top three to the entire team. List each group's ideas on a flip chart and use dot voting or another method to come to consensus on the most strategic operations. This exercise can refine and reshape the list of critical issues or suggest goals and objectives that will support critical issues.

PRIORITIZING CRITICAL ISSUES

Template 10: Strategic Priorities Quadrant is a tool for ranking the issues that have emerged to date and are temporarily "parked" in **Template 6: Critical Issues Inventory**. The simple quadrant format allows the team to assess each critical issue along two dimensions: significance and urgency. The scales that run from left to right and bottom to top identify two levels of significance and urgency: low and high. The underlying questions this matrix poses are:

- How *significant* is this issue for the success and sustainability of the institution?
- How *urgent* is this issue in terms of requiring immediate, short-term, or long-term attention?

Posing these questions requires the team to test each issue for significance and urgency in light of all its deliberations to date, especially those relating to mission and vision.

Once this matrix is filled in, the team will be able to identify the most critical issues by their location. The numbers in each quadrant help the planning team to rank critical issues. Moving from highest to lowest priority:

- The numeral 1 in the upper-right quadrant indicates that these issues are of greatest significance for the success and sustainability of the institution. Highly significant and urgent, they should probably be addressed within the next six to twelve months.
- The numeral 2 in the upper-left quadrant signals that these are the next most important issues—highly significant but of lesser urgency, suggesting a time frame of one to two years.
- The lower-right quadrant contains issues that are of relatively low strategic import but that nevertheless need to be dealt with in the near future (within six to twelve months).
- The lower-left quadrant contains issues that are of lower strategic priority and less urgency, so perhaps they can be eliminated or delegated for relatively simple resolution.

TEMPLATE 10: STRATEGIC PRIORITIES QUADRANT

Prioritize Critical Issues

In the matrix below, allocate the critical issues identified in **Template 6: Critical Issues Inventory**. Determine the most appropriate quadrant by thinking of where each issue falls on the scale of significance and urgency.

URGENCY

		LOW		HIGH
		2: High Significance/Low Urgency Issues crucial for institutional success/survival but not urgent (1–2-year time frame)		**1: High Significance/High Urgency** Issues crucial for institutional success/survival and urgent (6–12-month time frame)
HIGH	HL1		HH1	
	HL2		HH2	
	HL3		HH3	
	HL4		HH4	
	HL5		HH5	
	HL6		HH6	
	HL7		HH7	
	HL8		HH8	
	HL9		HH9	
	HL10		HH10	
		4: Low Significance/Low Urgency Issues of relatively low strategic significance and urgency (not necessary to address)		**3: Low Significance/High Urgency** Issues not crucial for institutional success/survival but urgent (6–12-month time frame)
LOW	LL1		LH1	
	LL2		LH2	
	LL3		LH3	
	LL4		LH4	
	LL5		LH5	
	LL6		LH6	
	LL7		LH7	
	LL8		LH8	
	LL9		LH9	
	LL10		LH10	

SIGNIFICANCE

The placement of each issue requires a subjective judgment call. Most issues do not fall neatly into a simple low-high framework; however, this template is a useful tool that forces a greater degree of discrimination in light of mission and vision. As an example, imagine that a particular museum identifies the following critical issue early in its strategic planning process: *Increase awareness of the museum and use of its resources by local school district administrators and teachers.* Is this strategically significant? If the mission and vision statements emphasize an educational purpose and a strong commitment to community outreach, then yes. If, however, they focus on the preservation of objects or the advancement of research in a particular field, the issue is less significant.

DEVELOPING STRATEGIC INITIATIVES

Having analyzed the critical issues in the preceding exercises, the Strategic Planning Team is now in a position to identify those that will evolve into strategic initiatives and form the framework of the strategic plan. A strategic initiative is a broad but coherent approach to realize the museum's mission and vision with available resources. It suggests a general direction rather than a specific course of action. While strategic initiatives can adapt to changing circumstances, they are not hastily changed. Each of these broad approaches might be thought of as the trunk of a tree, from which grows large branches (goals) and eventually smaller branches and leaves (objectives).

Template 11 has two parts: **Template 11A: Strategic Initiatives Worksheet** and **Template 11B: Goals and Objectives Worksheet**. This is the critical stage where the work that has been done to date gets translated into a single template. Template 11A records the evolution of the team's strategic thinking from **Template 9: SWOT Matrix** to **Template 10: Strategic Priorities Quadrant**, leading to the identification of strategic initiatives. Template 11B further defines the initiatives by articulating specific goals and objectives and assigning responsibility and time frames to each.

One way to identify strategic initiatives is to review the activities generated by applying applicative, transformative, additive, and subtractive thinking to the SWOTs. Identify the most promising idea in each operation, and list it in the first column of Template 11A. Another technique is to look at the critical issues that were identified as priorities in Template 10. Start with the issues that landed in the upper-right quadrant, then shift to those in the upper left, and finally those in the lower right. Insert the top priorities in the second column. Applying both techniques will help to sharpen the focus on issues that have been on the Strategic Planning Team's radar screen.

Looking at the items in the first two columns for what they have in common will help the team to zero in on strategic initiatives that will shape the strategic plan. After coming to consensus on the gist of the initiatives, either the entire team or small groups should spend some time articulating them in clear and inspiring terms. Then list the strategic initiatives in the third column.

To illustrate how this thought process works, let's assume that a major weakness identified in the SWOT Matrix is a location that is not easily accessible to a key population group. An applicative strategy to overcome this weakness might be to collaborate with local/regional mass transit to improve access to the museum. This SWOT-derived strategy would be listed in column 1 of the Strategic Initiatives Worksheet. Let's also assume that the High Significance/High Urgency quadrant of the Strategic Priorities Matrix identifies addressing increasing criticism of the museum by this same population group, which represents an important constituency. This Strategic Priorities strategy would be listed in column 2. Taken together, these two insights might lead the Strategic Planning Team to articulate a strategic initiative in column 3: *Increase outreach to underserved communities.* Notice that the initiative is stated in sufficiently broad terms to encompass this particular population as well as any others that might also be underserved. Using Template 11B, the Strategic Planning Team can identify a set of goals and objectives for this strategic initiative, such as identifying and adding new locations to pick up visitors in their neighborhoods and drop them off at the museum and modifying the schedule during festivals and other special events.

This same interplay between the SWOT strategic thinking and the prioritization of critical issues can give rise to all sorts of strategic initiatives. It is a process of integration and synthesis that can't be reduced to a simple formula, but, as the above example suggests, it can result in creative thinking, collaboration, and consensus building around strategically significant initiatives, goals, and objectives.

The strategic initiatives in the third column of Template 11A will automatically appear in the first column of Template 11B. For each initiative, the team will brainstorm goals that support it. After selecting the most strategic and viable goals, they'll be listed in the second column. A goal is an outcome statement that tells how the museum

TEMPLATE 11A: STRATEGIC INITIATIVES WORKSHEET

Use **Template 9: SWOT Matrix** to complete the strategic thinking lists.

Use **Template 10: Strategic Priorities Quadrant** to identify prioritized issues.

Enter strategic initiatives in the third column. Note that this language is copied throughout the templates.

Strategic Thinking	Prioritized Issues	Strategic Initiatives
Strengths v. Weaknesses	1: High Significance/High Urgency	Strategic Initiative 1
Strengths v. Threats		
		Strategic Initiative 2
Weakness > Strength	2: High Significance/Low Urgency	
Threats > Opportunities		
		Strategic Initiative 3
Strength + Strength	3: Low Significance/High Urgency	
Opportunity + Opportunity		Strategic Initiative 4
Weakness – Weakness		
		Strategic Initiative 5
Threat – Threat		

TEMPLATE 11B: GOALS AND OBJECTIVES WORKSHEET

Strategic Initiatives	Goals	Objectives	Responsibility	Time Frame
Initiative 1 Integrate the museum into academics, research, and student life on campus	A. Increase curricular connections with a broad spectrum of academic departments	1. Establish an academic advisory board	Director of academic programs; chair of natural sciences dept.	Fall semester 2018
		2. Provide mini-grants to faculty to develop new ways to use the museum for teaching classes	Director of academic programs; academic advisory board	2019–2020 academic year
		3. Strategize with administration about the role the museum can play in university efforts to recruit science majors	Executive director; director of marketing	Spring semester 2019

will address, resolve, or accomplish a strategic initiative. In short, it articulates what will be accomplished. More fluid than strategic initiatives, goals can be adjusted and adapted with changing circumstances.

For example, a university natural history museum might identify a strategic initiative to: *integrate the museum into academics, research, and student life on campus.* From there, it could identify three goals to support the initiative:

A. Increase curricular connections with a broad spectrum of academic departments.
B. Become a resource for researchers who want to incorporate outreach components in their work.
C. Create programs that make the museum a draw for students in various academic disciplines.

Using Goal 1A as an example, Template 11B shows how it is realized through specific objectives, listed in column 3, responsibilities in column 4, and time frames in column 5. An objective is a precise, measurable, time-phased result that supports the achievement of a goal. It spells out how the goal will be accomplished and often at whom the efforts are directed.

For example, objectives that support Strategic Initiative 1, Goal A, might include:

1A1. Establish an academic advisory board
1A2. Provide mini-grants to faculty to develop new ways to use the museum for teaching classes
1A3. Strategize with administration about the role the museum can play in university efforts to recruit science majors

For each objective to be realized, there must be an assignment of responsibility and a time frame. In the fourth column, list the individual or group that will take responsibility for each objective. In the fifth column, estimate the projected start and completion dates. These items will appear again in **Template 17: Operating Plan Report**.

MAKING ROOM FOR NEW INITIATIVES

Additive thinking plays a big part in strategic planning, as the Strategic Planning Team and staff members consider layer upon layer of new programs and services to accomplish the goals and objectives that support the strategic initiatives. Subtractive thinking is also needed to analyze current programs and eliminate those that do not advance the mission, are no longer supported by the community, or overtax the capacities of staff and museum facilities. We often hear the term "zero-based budgeting"; museum staff members also need to think in terms of zero-based programming. Conducting an objective and unbiased assessment of current programs and services can present a real challenge to staff members and volunteers, who naturally are very invested in existing programs. As one director observed, "I think the staff are experiencing the inherent contradiction of strategic planning. Part of the process involves thinking big as if there were no limits, and part of it requires a hard look at the real limitations."

Schedule a special staff meeting to lay the groundwork for program assessment. In museums with large staffs that offer many different types of programs and services, it may be necessary to divide into several teams that will report back to the larger group. Have a dialogue about the need to make room for healthy new growth, perhaps asking for examples from staff members' personal and professional lives.

Distinguish between outputs and outcomes and ask staff members to give examples of both in their own work (see definitions on p. 27). Examples of outputs are *Presented 725 tours serving 21,000 students* and *Developed new labels for local history exhibit*. Examples of outcomes are *Change in students' attitudes as reported by teachers* and *Increase in visitors' participation in community forums*. Emphasize the importance of thinking in terms of outcomes, especially for target audiences that are not currently being served.

Stephen Weil explains that the museum "can only convert its output—programs—into its desired bottom-line outcome—a beneficial impact—if there is a potential audience that finds its offerings to have value."[1] This concept is central to the board's responsibility to prescribe the museum's institutional focus. Weil quotes Harold Skramstad, who says that a clear and focused statement of institutional mission meets two critical needs. Not only does it serve as a guide to institutional action, but it also functions as "a powerful yardstick against which the museum can assess each and every activity it carries out."[2] With a clear definition of institutional focus and a directive to realign resources from the board, staff will be better able to eliminate or consolidate current programs that no longer serve a strategic purpose or make the best use of available resources.

To make these difficult decisions, the staff must evaluate each current offering relative to others. While every program has impact, the challenge is to determine which have the greatest impact. To do that, consider the following questions about each program or service the museum offers:

- How, and to what degree, does this program support the mission when compared with other programs currently offered?
- How, and to what degree, does this program advance specific strategic initiatives?
- How much staff and volunteer time does this program require, and what is its impact on our audiences?
- What financial and physical resources are required, and what is the return on investment?
- Considering net revenue, how could this program be more cost effective?
- How can outcomes of this program be measured in terms of our audiences? What are the benchmarks of success?
- How many people are served by this program, and what is the type and degree of impact?
- Does this program contribute to a sense of community for the museum?
- What growth strategy—increase, maintain, decrease, or eliminate—is recommended for each program and why?

The last question is of critical importance because, as any gardener knows, healthy growth requires pruning. If the staff recommends maintaining or increasing the majority of existing programs, that leaves little room for growth. Remember, a well-crafted mission statement and a clear institutional focus will help the institution decide what it needs to start doing, what it needs to continue doing, and what it needs to stop doing in order to move forward. With consensus around mission and strategic initiatives, it is unlikely that staff or board members would promote favorite programs that do not support the agreed-upon strategic direction.

TAKE NOTE!
- Strategic plans are generally organized with a logical sequence of statements, going from the most general or conceptual to the more tactical. The templates in this book outline plans with three layers of statements: strategic initiatives, goals, and objectives. Planning teams may elect to use a different vocabulary. Whatever the terminology, statements should be written at a consistent level of specificity. Some plans include overarching ideas (sometimes termed "strategies" or "new directions") that are not explicitly tied to the sequence of implementation statements. While these big ideas are inspiring, they must, in some way, be tied to the sequence of actions if they are to be achieved.
- Dot voting is an effective and versatile method that uses color-coded file labels available at office supply stores to identify a group's collective priorities. Give all participants the same number of dots (based on the group size), the number of options, and the number of rankings, and then ask them to place the dots on their highest priorities. In addition to counting the number of dots on each option, colors can be used to indicate level of priority and who is casting votes. It is a good idea to clarify whether participants can place more than one dot on a single issue.
- In Template 11B and throughout the rest of the linked templates (12, 14, 15, 16, and 17), there are links that automatically move information between the spreadsheets. Those cells are shaded light gray. As the team completes each template, text or numbers will be transferred to other templates. To preserve these links, the spreadsheets should all be saved in a single folder, and the file names cannot be changed. When opening any of these templates, users will see a dialogue box; always select the option of updating links.

NOTES

1. Stephen E. Weil, "Are You Really Worth What You Cost or Just Merely Worthwhile? And Who Gets to Say?" accessed February 25, 2018, https://www.issuelab.org/resources/8291/8291.pdf.

2. Ibid.

Phase 5

Develop Performance Measures

With the completion of Phase 4, the framework of the strategic plan has been built, from initiatives to goals to objectives. If this approach focused only on strategic planning, now would be the time to write the plan and consider the work completed. The written document will be addressed in Phase 7 (Report and Monitor). But since this approach encompasses strategic thinking and planning, it provides tools to ensure that the thinking that has gone into creating the plan goes on to measure the results.

Measuring performance in light of institutional mission and strategy often calls for new indicators. The team needs to ask: What does the board consider the top three measures of success? How integral are these measures to the new plan? In the words of Peter Drucker, "You need to remind yourself again and again that the results of a nonprofit institution are always outside the organization, not inside."[1] How does the museum know whether it is being successful in meeting new visitor-centered goals? Two templates will help the Strategic Planning Team, staff, and board members to answer this critical question.

- **Template 12: Performance Indicators Inventory** is a table that will help the Strategic Planning Team develop performance indicators to measure success in achieving specific goals that support strategic initiatives.
- **Template 13: Strategic Dashboard Framework** is a list of factors that will be useful to board and staff leaders charged with monitoring institutional performance. It also includes guidelines and examples for staff members who will be charged with creating visual displays of strategic performance indicators.

THE VALUE OF OUTCOME MEASUREMENT

The process of developing a mission statement involved thinking in terms of the museum's *outcomes*, not merely its *outputs*. Like mission and vision, performance measurement must take outcomes into account. Museums have found the issue of outcome measurement particularly challenging because so much of what they are about is intangible, subjective, and long term. Nevertheless, they must demonstrate their relevance to the communities they serve and their worthiness to the funders who provide financial support. In these days of expanding leisure-time options and shrinking revenues, museums are often asked, "How does what you do make a difference to those you serve?" To answer this difficult question, they must use persuasive metrics that demonstrate their value.

In his keynote address at the Museum Trustee Association's Assembly 2002, Stephen E. Weil, scholar emeritus at the Smithsonian's Center for Education and Museum Studies, charged board members with the responsibility to monitor and assure their museum's institutional performance. Carrying out this responsibility requires "timely and accurate assessment of the museum's actual impact on its target audiences." Realizing that there are few established methods for measuring their impact, Weil challenged museums to "develop not just a few but a whole arsenal—a vast arsenal, even—of richer and more persuasive ways by which museums can document and/or demonstrate the myriad and beneficial outcomes that they are able to achieve."[2] These measures will help museum leaders think and act strategically while benefiting their institutions, the communities they serve, and the profession at large.

Weil cited Peter Frumkin, professor of public policy at the John F. Kennedy School of Government, Harvard University, who suggests that nonprofits measure their "programmatic bottom line" rather than relying on financial measures to determine their effectiveness. Frumkin explains that "nonprofit groups of all kinds . . . are understandably led to focus on financial measures of performance because they are so much more concrete and robust than programmatic ones. They are also what outsiders can observe easily and compare quickly in sizing up one organization's management compared with another."[3]

Herein may lay the crux of the matter: to measure an organization's effectiveness in serving its audience's needs does not require comparison with other organizations. It requires comparison of the organization's goals with the audience's experience. Such assessments are unique to each institution and to each community. And it is in exactly this arena where each institution must succeed or fail. As Weil points out, museums are not about "dollars and cents" but "hearts and minds." Measuring their impact on human beings calls for assessment techniques to be "smartened up to fit the real complexity of what museums actually do."[4]

ASSESSING OUTCOMES OF INITIATIVES THAT CANNOT BE MEASURED QUANTITATIVELY

Often the most significant benefits museums provide to the communities they serve are the most difficult to measure. Like a seed that takes root and doesn't grow into a tree for years, the experience of seeing an original work of art or an authentic historical document can ultimately have a profound impact on a visitor's life, inspiring a new avocation or even a change in vocation. But how does a museum measure the highly personal, sometimes emotional, and often long-term impacts of museum visits?

Although it requires a leap forward in evaluation methodology, museums must start somewhere to measure visitor-centered outcomes that are tied to their deepest values and purpose. There is no magic formula for determining appropriate performance measures. Some will be so obvious that the strategic goals virtually define them—for example, a goal to increase museum membership by 20 percent would naturally call for keeping a close eye on membership figures and their levels from month to month. At the other end of the spectrum are some very important, mission-driven goals that may be extremely difficult to measure. If the museum's mission is to enhance the public's understanding of an era or event on which opinions are deeply divided, how can it define a meaningful metric for such inherently intangible goals, much less do the measuring?

Some outcomes or impacts are so subtle or subjective as to render the whole idea of measurement suspect. This is where the value of quantitative versus qualitative data comes into play. To say that a goal can be measured is not to say that it can be quantified. Nevertheless, it is possible to apply rigorous thinking to indicators that are largely intangible. Identifying important questions and posing them in a systematic fashion makes it possible to gauge visitors' reactions and measure the museum's impact. Combining rigor with creativity and involving staff and volunteers at all levels of the organizational structure can lead to the development of new approaches to measuring qualitative data. For example, conducting pre- and post-tests with visitors to a special exhibition makes it possible to capture their names so the museum can stay in touch with them. Monitoring attitudes and behaviors over time is especially relevant in measuring the impact of the kinds of profound experiences that can occur in museums. It also provides the valuable dividend of demonstrating a sustained interest in public value.

Some of the most revealing evidence of institutional impact and perceived benefit (or lack thereof) can be found in visitor comments. The key to using anecdotal information for developing meaningful insights is the methodology for collecting, codifying, and analyzing feedback. Information collected regularly and methodically is far more valuable than that gathered sporadically and analyzed selectively. Narrative comments can be solicited from key audiences through the museum's website, social media, touch-screen kiosks, comment cards, exit interviews, email surveys, and focus groups. They can then be coded in ways that speak to mission and strategy issues. For example, consider using the SWOT framework to codify visitor comments about a temporary exhibit or a new program and report the findings at a board retreat.

The mission statement developed in Phase 2 (Clarify Mission, Vision, and Values) should have its own metrics—mission metrics—that transform it from being merely a banner used to rally the troops to an instrument of ongoing leadership and management. Like the armature within a sculpture, the mission statement is the core of the entire enterprise. Successive layers of exhibitions, programs, and services may lend the museum its external form, but this central statement determines its basic shape.

Using the mission statement of the University Museum of Natural History as an example, table 5.1 arrays a set of performance indicators that respond to each phrase of a mission statement. As this "armature" format illustrates, the component phrases—developed in Phase 2 through in-depth consideration of purpose, audience, methods, and impacts—can now guide the Strategic Planning Team in determining appropriate performance measures. Beneath each phrase of the mission statement are spaces to describe performance indicators—qualitative or quantitative—that most appropriately measure the phrase. To use the armature format as a report, graphic displays, ratios, other numeric values, and narrative bullet points can be inserted in the space beneath each phrase.

Table 5.1

Mission Statement			
Purpose	Community	Methods	Impacts
The University Museum of Natural History tells the story of our planet and its inhabitants . . .	to families and students of all ages . . .	through artifacts, specimens, and programs that reveal the process of scientific research and discovery . . .	showing how university scientists answer current questions while raising new ones.

Performance Indicators			
Number of exhibits and programs that use stories and engaging narratives Diversity of human cultures and other living species featured in these stories	Percent of admissions, memberships, and other participants who are families and students, by age	Visitor recall of lessons learned about the scientific method of inquiry Use of collection of specimens and artifacts for demonstrations of scientific investigation	Involvement of university scientists in presenting current research agendas and areas of further investigation

EXAMPLES OF PERFORMANCE INDICATORS FOR MUSEUMS

While there are conventional metrics that are regularly monitored by board and staff leaders, the creation of a new strategic plan provides an opportunity to consider new frameworks on which performance measures can be built. These may be thought of in terms of "survival" issues, which tend to have financial implications, and "mission" issues, which are often more visitor centered. Another potential framework is "mission monitors," which measure how well an institution is living up to its purpose, and "means monitors," which measure efficiency.

Expanding upon these dualistic approaches, John Jacobsen, in his book *Measuring Museum Impact and Performance*, has identified four categories of impact with fourteen subcategories. The following are derived from 1,025 indicators gathered from fifty-one sources.[5]

Public Impacts
- Broadening participation
- Preserving heritage
- Strengthening social capital
- Enhancing public knowledge
- Serving education
- Advancing social change
- Communicating public identity and image

Private Impacts
- Contributing to the economy
- Delivering corporate community services

Personal Impacts
- Enabling personal growth
- Offering personal respite
- Welcoming personal leisure

Institutional Impacts
- Helping museum operations
- Building museum capital

Jacobsen cautions that "achieving certain metrics should not become the de facto purpose of a museum. Rather, the museum needs to actually improve the world, and to select metrics that are meaningful indicators of its achievements."[6]

After choosing the framework that will be used and identifying the specific performance indicators that are most relevant to the museum and its strategic goals, the next step is to set a normative value or level for the particular measure that is consistent with each goal. For example, if the indicator is "growth in attendance," the normative value may be 10 percent growth year to year. This part of the exercise will be more or less challenging, depending on the specificity of the measure and the degree to which it is quantitative rather than qualitative. It is best to set such a value after the museum has gained some experience in collecting data for the indicator in question.

THINKING STRATEGICALLY ABOUT PERFORMANCE INDICATORS

Template 12: Performance Indicators Inventory will help the Strategic Planning Team start to organize its thinking about the measurement of goals that support strategic initiatives. This simple table is designed to identify appropriate metrics for each goal. As in previous templates, it includes five strategic initiatives and allows for five goals to support each one.

TEMPLATE 12: PERFORMANCE INDICATORS INVENTORY

Strategic Initiative 1	Goals	Performance Indicators
Integrate the museum into academics, research, and student life on campus	A. Increase curricular connections with a broad spectrum of academic departments	Number of new courses that utilize the museum exhibitions and collections in instruction Diversity of academic departments interacting with museum staff members
	B. Become a resource for researchers who want to incorporate outreach components in their work	Number of researchers who share current research with museum audiences The variety of presentation formats used by researchers
	C. Create programs that make the museum a draw for students in various academic disciplines	Student attendance figures Diversity of student majors

To start the conversation, ask Strategic Planning Team members to envision performance measures that might be used in gauging achievement of these goals. Discuss various assessment techniques, information sources, or specific performance indicators, choosing those that are most relevant and achievable. Distinguish between qualitative and quantitative information and indicate where one would be a more useful measure than another.

Template 12 progresses from the university museum's initiative to better integrate itself with academics and student life (in the first column) to specific goals (column 2) and performance indicators for each goal (column 3). The performance indicators move from outputs such as number of researchers, to outcomes, such as variety of presentation formats.

REPORTING ON ACHIEVEMENT OF STRATEGIC INITIATIVES

As observed by the Cheshire Cat in *Alice in Wonderland*, if someone doesn't know (or care) where they are going, any road will take them there. Knowing the museum's destination (strategic initiative) and having a road map to get there (goals and objectives), while essential, are not enough. The driver also needs road signs, speed and fuel gauges, and warning light indicators—external signals that indicate progress along the chosen path and internal signals that keep the driver constantly informed of the vehicle's speed, performance, and condition. Dashboard reports are an increasingly common and useful tool to help boards and senior managers focus their attention on what matters most. Ideally confined to a single page, this report format—like the instrument panel of a car—is a set of gauges and warning lights that assist the board in quickly assessing incremental progress toward the achievement of strategic initiatives. The goals and objectives supporting each initiative are monitored regularly, though the frequency may be monthly, quarterly, or annually. Because dashboard reports present key indicators in a consistent format that does not change from meeting to meeting, board members and staff leaders can readily spot changes and trends.

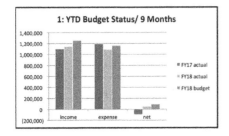

1: YTD Budget Status/ 9 Months — FY17 actual, FY18 actual, FY18 budget

2: Supporting Data

	FY17 actual	FY18 actual	FY18 budget
income	1,099,550	1,146,569	1,174,845
expense	1,193,264	1,090,188	1,162,444
net	(93,714)	56,381	12,401

Income Sources	FY18 budget	YTD budget	YTD actual
program	415,000	290,774	223,223
other earned	560,000	396,510	390,555
public support	89,000	61,679	75,250
investments	190,845	132,170	129,456

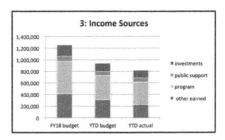

3: Income Sources — investments, public support, program, other earned

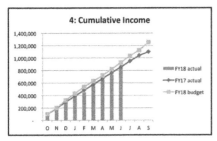

4: Cumulative Income — FY18 actual, FY17 actual, FY18 budget

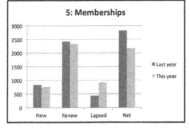

5: Memberships — Last year, This year

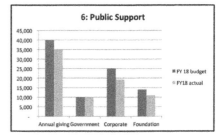

6: Public Support — FY 18 budget, FY18 actual

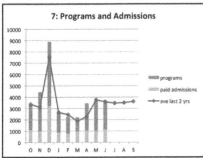

7: Programs and Admissions — programs, paid admissions, ave last 2 yrs

Highlights

5: Memberships - Total membership has declined over last year, from 2824 to 2179, a drop of 645 members or 23%. Over twice as many members lapsed (921 v 437).
Had the lapses remained at prior levels, membership would be 2663.
1: Budget Status: Income is ahead of last year but below budget. By controlling expenses, YTD net revenue is ahead of last year.
7: Programs: The December Open House drew more people than in the last two years. Evaluations indicate that the chamber quartet was a significant draw.
Also, the new Art for Your Garden event boosted April attendance.

FIGURE 5.1
Strategic Initiative Indicators (Courtesy of the Museum Trustee Association)

Figure 5.1 is an example of such a dashboard designed to inform the board of progress on the strategic initiative: *Build and Diversify Revenues.* At first glance, this report seems quite dense—a lot of numerical and graphic information is communicated on a single page. Looking at each window individually reveals multiple perspectives on the museum's progress. In window 1 in the upper-left corner, actual year-to-date revenues are compared to the current and prior year's budgets.

Window 3, in the upper-right corner, shows museum revenues by source. The numerical details for windows 1 and 3 are shown in the table in window 2. These three windows provide an example of how numerical data is translated into graphic terms. Since this museum is interested in expanding revenues from public support, this topic is examined further in other windows. Window 5 shows membership trends over two years; window 6 breaks down the sources of public support. The placement of window 4 (with its monthly display of cumulative income versus budgeted income) above window 7 (which displays the monthly visits this year versus the average of the past two years) permits the eye to see whether there are relationships between attendance levels and income. This juxtaposition illustrates the importance of layout in the design of dashboards.

Throughout the dashboard there is an attempt to provide comparisons—actual versus budget, current year versus previous year, actual new memberships versus goal. These and other comparisons give the board a context for extracting meaning from the data—in essence, converting data into strategic information. The window on the lower right is reserved for words to report highlights and explain key points revealed by the data. Each point is bulleted with the window number it refers to.

As valuable as these measures and formats are, Larry Butler cautions that they "are not the end product of organizational or program evaluation but the top layer—the high-level view that points board and staff to where they might need to drill down into a more detailed, refined understanding of organizational and program effectiveness."[7]

Template 13: Strategic Dashboard Framework is a compilation of different types of data and data displays that can be used to monitor progress in achieving strategic initiatives. It is sometimes helpful to create reports that focus on selected initiatives rather than including all of them in a single dashboard. The following types of data displays can be tailored to a variety of strategic initiatives.

- *Performance versus budget.* In Phase 6 (Develop Operating Plan and Budgets), strategic initiatives become the organizing framework for building the museum's operating budget and can thus be measured in terms of actual performance against budget.
- *Component analysis.* Looking at the share of a total quantity represented by one component of that quantity—such as the percentage of total revenues represented by public support or the share of students in a community who have been visitors—is a common and often useful way of viewing performance, especially in comparison to prior periods, an established goal, or the analogous performance of peer institutions.
- *Ratio analysis.* Relating a numerator to a denominator—such as costs per visitor or current assets to current liabilities—can reveal aspects of operating efficiency, productivity, financial condition, or institutional effectiveness.
- *Year-to-year change.* Annual changes in membership, paid attendance, gift shop income, and public satisfaction scores provide a sense of short-term direction, positive or negative, that can help managers focus on areas needing immediate attention.
- *Monthly performance.* Museum visitation and other phenomena that may change seasonally or periodically can be observed in calendar-based graphic displays, especially when juxtaposed with other monthly displays.
- *Board participation.* Lists of board activities and time devoted to each can provide evidence of the active involvement of board members in advancing the museum's mission.
- *Staff and volunteer participation.* Similarly, lists of staff and volunteer activities, such as gathering data on visitor-centered outcomes, can be evidence of the commitment of staff members and volunteers to supporting strategic goals.
- *Collections use.* Records of how the collection is used—not only for exhibitions but also for individual research and behind-the-scenes opportunities—can reveal ways the collections are used to support the mission and advance strategic initiatives.

Every board chair and director has metrics that are traditionally kept on their radar screens, be they the proverbial bottom line or indicators on a new initiative or pet project. Since those who are not so familiar with a particular type of reporting are less inclined to value established metrics, they are often in a good position to suggest new indicators for measuring institutional effectiveness. Engaging in blue-sky thinking with staff members from departments across the museum may suggest valuable additions to established metrics.

A look back to figure 0.14 on page xxiv provides a reminder that Phase 5 (Develop Performance Measures) falls within the realm of board responsibility. As reported in *Museum Board Leadership 2017*, directors and board chairs gave their boards a grade of B- when it comes to adopting and following a strategic plan,[8] suggesting that there is

TEMPLATE 13: STRATEGIC DASHBOARD FRAMEWORK

There is no one-size-fits-all dashboard. Each is unique to the museum, its mission, vision, strategic initiatives, goals, and objectives. The clearer it is to the board and staff members who will refer to it, the more valuable it is.

Frameworks

There are many frameworks that can be utilized to measure outcomes. Each can be used as a scaffold for helping an institution determine how well its resources and programs are being used to meet strategic goals. Whatever approach is chosen, a dashboard can be a helpful tool for monitoring progress on a regular basis. Here are three useful frameworks, each looking through different lenses:

John Jacobsen, *Measuring Museum Impact and Performance*	Laura Roberts, *Monitoring Performance with a Dashboard*	Larry Butler, *The Nonprofit Dashboard: Using Metrics to Drive Mission Success*
▪ Public ▪ Private ▪ Personal ▪ Institutional	▪ Comparables ▪ Averages ▪ Strategic goals ▪ History	▪ Mission metrics ▪ Strategic initiatives ▪ Risk factors ▪ Outcomes

Indicators

Consider the appropriateness of lagging indicators versus leading indicators. When reporting on financial data, which is reported in the past, remember that it cannot predict what's going to happen in the future. Stakeholder feedback, however, is suggestive—though not definitive—regarding future behavior.

Programs	Revenues—sufficient/ sustainable in each of the following?	Stakeholders— external and internal
▪ Advance mission and vision ▪ In sync with strategic initiatives, goals, and objectives ▪ Supported by the communities they aim to serve	▪ Programs ▪ Earned income ▪ Public support ▪ Investments ▪ Grants	▪ Attendance ▪ Membership ▪ Community collaborations ▪ Staff ▪ Board ▪ Volunteers

Steps

1. Choose approach.

2. Identify performance indicators, including outcomes as well as outputs, qualitative as well as quantitative. Even in today's computerized cars, dashboards only have so many indicators. A manageable number is somewhere between five and ten.

3. Establish frequency of measurement and time frames.

4. Explore data available for each indicator, looking internally and among sister institutions.

5. Establish benchmarks and set normative values.

6. Collect data and explore different ways to present it. Get input from board and staff leaders and revise based on feedback.

7. Experiment with a variety of formats.

8. Pilot with key board and staff members.

9. Present at board and staff meetings and revise as needed. When people are familiar with this presentation, maintain the basic format, updating data as called for by evolution of plan.

10. Update monthly, quarterly, or annually as appropriate for various indicators and stakeholders.

Methods

- Provide comparisons (e.g., goals vs. actual)

- Progressions showing trends (e.g., year to year—up, down, or flat)

- Component analysis

- Brief notations included to emphasize key metrics

- Visitor comments—analyze and code. (See example of responses to open-ended question on Strategic Planning Team Survey, page 23.)

- Social media metrics (e.g., Trip Advisor, Facebook, Twitter)

Formats

Display techniques—consistency builds familiarity and makes it easier to spot patterns and trends (applies to graphics, locations, names, acronyms, etc.)

Color coding or shading, depending on whether color or black-and-white printer

Symbols

Different styles and sizes of fonts

Basic styles illustrated in text: mission metrics (table 5.1); combination of graphic, numerical, and narrative (figure 5.1)

To learn more, see:

- Lawrence Butler, *The Nonprofit Dashboard: Using Metrics to Drive Mission Success*

- John Jacobsen, *Measuring Museum Impact and Performance*

- Laura Roberts, *Monitoring Performance with a Dashboard* (https://www.lauraroberts.com/ideas.html)

room for improvement in this area. To fulfill their fiduciary responsibility, board members must not only approve the plan but also conceptualize what following it will look like. They can do this by first identifying the most relevant indicators and then establishing acceptable norms. This role is among their most important as lay governors. It is the essence of strategic thinking in operation.

TAKE NOTE!

- In Template 12, there are links that automatically transfer information from Templates 11A and 11B. Those cells are shaded light gray. As the team completes each template, text or numbers will be transferred to subsequent templates. To preserve these links, the spreadsheets should all be saved in a single folder, and the file names cannot be changed.

NOTES

1. Peter F. Drucker, *The Five Most Important Questions You Will Ever Ask about Your Nonprofit Organization* (San Francisco: Jossey-Bass, 1993), 50.

2. Stephen E. Weil, "Are You Really Worth What You Cost or Just Merely Worthwhile? And Who Gets to Say?" accessed February 25, 2018, https://www.issuelab.org/resources/8291/8291.pdf.

3. Ibid.

4. Ibid.

5. John W. Jacobsen, *Measuring Museum Impact and Performance* (Lanham, MD: Rowman & Littlefield, 2016), 14.

6. Ibid., 37.

7. Lawrence Butler, *The Nonprofit Dashboard: A Tool for Tracking Progress* (Washington, DC: BoardSource), 2.

8. BoardSource, *Museum Board Leadership 2017: A National Report* (Washington, DC: BoardSource, 2017), 19.

Phase 6

Develop Operating Plan and Budgets

This phase represents a critical juncture between strategic planning and budgeting. In order to realize the goals and objectives outlined in the plan, the board and staff must integrate them into the museum's budgeting process. Unfortunately, because established practices don't often mesh with new initiatives, strategic plans often unravel at this decisive point. Updating traditional budget frameworks by simply inserting new line items does not create an effective link between strategic and operating plans. Incorporating input from staff and board, the templates in this phase are designed to develop new budgeting processes that will create that crucial strategic link.

Having established strategic initiatives, goals, and objectives in Phase 4 (Determine Strategies), the Strategic Planning Team must now bring in staff members to add substance and details to the plan it has created. Trustees also have an essential role to play. To provide guidance to staff, the board (or a committee thereof) must ask: How should financial resources be aligned with strategic priorities? What options do we have to reallocate existing resources or generate additional resources? The work of Phase 6 is an exercise that is set in motion by the Strategic Planning Team and completed by the staff and the board. It translates broad strategic commitments into an operational plan that ties directly into the museum's operating and capital budgets.

The templates introduced in this chapter are designed to integrate strategic initiatives into the budgeting process. They are not a substitute for traditional departmental budgeting but a way to view budgeting through the lens of strategy.

- **Template 14: Operating Plan Worksheets** asks the Strategic Planning Team, with input from staff, to estimate in global terms the financial and human resources required to achieve the goals and objectives for each strategic initiative defined in Phase 4.
- **Template 15: Cost and Revenue Worksheets** will help staff members in various departments to convert these global estimates into a more detailed set of cost and revenue projections.
- **Template 16: Multiyear Budget Worksheets** will be used to project costs and revenue for initiatives that extend over the term of the strategic plan.

THE IMPORTANCE OF LINKING BUDGETS TO STRATEGY

All too often, strategic thinking simply fades into the background as the strategic plan is completed and the traditional budgeting process takes over. All links between strategic and operating plans are lost when conventional thinking, with its internal focus on established practices and departmental agendas, prevails over strategic thinking.

Strategic initiatives are generally institution-wide in scope, cutting across departmental and functional boundaries. Operating budgets, on the other hand, tend to be structured within these very boundaries. They also employ cost and revenue line items that are more reflective of fieldwide practice than institutional goals or strategic initiatives, which are unique to each museum. In short, they reflect old priorities and practices rather than new directions.

The templates in this chapter will help avoid this ineffective disconnect between strategic planning and budgeting by helping museum leaders to think—and act—strategically. As the most significant control tool available to institutional leadership, the annual budget is a critical factor in the decision-making of board and staff members alike. And since most institutions refer to their budgets with much greater frequency than to their strategic plans, this critical connection will keep the strategic plan in the forefront of the minds of internal stakeholders.

The benefit of linking the strategic plan to operations in a single, seamless planning-budgeting process is clear. For starters, it saves time by avoiding duplicative processes. The executive director of a museum that links its strategic plan to individual performance appraisals as a first step said, "I did not want to create a separate, parallel process; I simply came to this from the perspective of efficiency." This technique will also help managers think differently about human and financial resources. In short, it will transform the way they manage.

It will also make the difference between a strategic plan that is filed away and one that is achieved. Far too many strategic plans include bold and innovative initiatives that are never realized because those charged with envisioning them are not the ones responsible for finding the necessary resources and monitoring expenses. The process outlined in this chapter brings together those who serve on the Strategic Planning Team and those who serve on the board and staff to work together to actually implement the plan. This is a good time to start expanding the group because the greater the participation in shaping and fine-tuning individual components, the greater the investment in achieving the overall plan.

THE PREMISES OF INTEGRATING STRATEGY AND BUDGETING

The budget projections developed with Templates 14, 15, and 16 will serve as a reality test of the initial global estimates and, with refinement, will become the basis of the operating and capital budgets. The Strategic Planning Team shapes the process by thinking in global terms about the type and scale of resources required to realize the strategic initiatives they have already defined. Staff members at various levels will work out the details. A look back at figure 0.15 shows that the development of the operating plan falls within the realm of staff responsibilities. The templates are organized as a two-step exercise based on the following principles:

- Costs are examined in **Template 15: Cost and Revenue Worksheets**, first without consideration of the revenues required to cover them. Then revenue generation and fund development issues are added into the equation.
- The budget time frame is linked to the length of the strategic plan. So a three-year plan requires budgeting three years out, using **Template 16: Multiyear Budget Worksheets**. While this budget will be less precise than an annual budget, it can be revised from year to year.
- Strategic initiatives drive the thought process and remain visibly linked to budget numbers and documentation.
- The process is an iterative exercise in which initial assumptions are modified in light of subsequent insights gained through more detailed examination of cost elements and revenue requirements.

ALIGNING RESOURCES WITH STRATEGIC INITIATIVES

Although the entire Strategic Planning Team was instrumental in envisioning the strategic plan, a newly formed task force can take the first step of integrating strategic initiatives with the budget. It should include team members who have the interest and experience to estimate the human and financial resources that are called for in each initiative. Bringing in staff members with experience in specific areas of operations and programs will be advantageous at this stage.

Template 14: Operating Plan Worksheets is linked to the Excel files in Templates 11A and 11B. There is one sheet for each of five initiatives, which should be adequate for most plans. The goals, objectives, assignment of responsibility, and anticipated time frame for each initiative are automatically transferred from Template 11B to columns 1–4 of Template 14. The budgeting task force must now fill in the resources required for each objective in column 5 and an estimated cost figure in column 6. (Some objectives may involve little in the way of financial expenditures—for example, those that call for significant volunteer involvement or in-kind contributions. If that is the case, make note of these resources in column 5, but leave column 6 blank.)

To illustrate how this works, return to the example of the strategic initiative for the university museum in Template 11B (*Integrate the museum into academics, research, and student life on campus*) and the first goal to accomplish that initiative (*Increase curricular connections with a broad spectrum of academic departments*). The resources needed for the first objective (*Establish an academic advisory board*) are limited to *staff time and minor budget allocation for meetings,* and in column 6 the incremental cost estimate is $400. The second objective is more ambitious and costly. *Provide mini-grants to faculty to develop new ways to use the museum for teaching classes* is

TEMPLATE 14: OPERATING PLAN WORKSHEETS

Strategic Initiative 1

Integrate the museum into academics, research, and student life on campus

Goals	Objectives	Responsibility	Time Frame	Resources Needed	Estimated Cost by Objective	Total Estimated Cost of Goal
A. Increase curricular connections with a broad spectrum of academic departments	1. Establish an academic advisory board	Director of academic programs; chair of natural sciences dept.	Fall semester 2018	staff time and minor budget allocation for meetings	$400	$8,900
	2. Provide mini-grants to faculty to develop new ways to use the museum for teaching classes	Director of academic programs; academic advisory board	2019–2020 and 2020–2021 academic years	$1,000 per grant; 2 grants per semester in 2 academic years; staff time to promote program, process applications	$8,000	
	3. Strategize with administration about the role the museum can play in university efforts to recruit science majors	Executive director; director of marketing	Spring semester 2019	staff time; reception during accepted students weekend in 2 academic years	$500	

anticipated to include two grants a semester in the second and third years of the plan. Based on a projection of $1,000 per grant, the cost estimate is $8,000. The third objective (*Strategize with administration about the role the museum can play in university efforts to recruit science majors*) requires staff time and budget for an anticipated reception for accepted students, at an incremental cost of $500. The total of all costs for this goal, $8,900, is automatically calculated in column 7.

This global cost estimate is automatically added to all the others for each strategic initiative; this rough approximation suggests each initiative's order of magnitude in terms of its financial implications for the institution. It may be necessary to go through this exercise several times to rethink the relative importance of particular initiatives, goals, and objectives to come up with cost estimates that seem reasonable. When the task force is satisfied with the way it has aligned estimated resources with strategic goals and objectives, staff members will take the next step.

DEVELOPING DETAILED COST AND REVENUE PROJECTIONS

The more accurate the projections of cost and revenue for each objective, the more likely they are to be met. Because they can draw on past experience with exhibits, programs, and services, staff members are in the best position to create detailed cost and revenue projections. Starting with the global dollar figures generated by the task force in Template 14, cross-departmental teams of staff members will use the Excel worksheets in **Template 15: Cost and Revenue Worksheets** to align the Strategic Planning Team's vision with the reality of the budget. The projected total costs of each goal from Template 14 are automatically entered on the "cost estimate" line of each worksheet in Template 15.

Template 15 contains six spreadsheets. The first is a summary of projected costs and revenue for each of the plan's initiatives. The cells in this spreadsheet contain formulas that are tied to the detailed spreadsheets that follow. These five sheets are designed to help staff members project the cost and revenues of each goal within the various initiatives.

Costs are detailed in two broad categories:

- *Operating costs* include staff, contractors or consultants, technology, materials development, marketing, research, evaluation, supplies, design and construction, maintenance contracts, training, fundraising, equipment, and other costs associated with specific programs, exhibitions, and services that advance a particular strategic initiative.
- *Capital costs* include expenditures for capital improvements—a new wing or exhibition space, a major accessioning program, or a significant repair. Because strategic plans so often involve significant one-time costs for new or renovated facilities, there is a separate category for these expenses. Each institution will set its own financial threshold for defining what constitutes a capital expenditure.

It is important to note that the worksheets ask staff members to identify *incremental* direct operating costs, not the full cost of each initiative and goal. Any program or project also incurs indirect costs from ongoing operations as well as overhead costs such as utilities, maintenance, and use of space. At some point, projects may require a detailed budget of all associated costs, particularly for grant proposals or other funding requests. However, at this point, the Strategic Planning Team is interested in determining the budgetary impact of the direct costs of the initiatives in the plan and how they might be funded.

As staff members complete their work in developing detailed budget projections, the spreadsheets will calculate the total costs for each budget category and for each goal. They will also calculate the difference between the initial estimated costs (from Template 14) and the more detailed revised projections on each spreadsheet. If the number

TEMPLATE 15: COST AND REVENUE WORKSHEETS

Strategic Initiative				
	Goal 1A	Goal 1B	Goal 1C	Total All Goals
Incremental Operating Costs				
additional, new staff				
contractors, consultants				
technology hardware and software				
materials development, design, and printing				
marketing				
research				
evaluation				
supplies				
exhibition or facilities design and construction				
maintenance contracts				
training and professional development				
fundraising				
equipment				
other 1				
other 2				
other 3				
other 4				
Total Operating Costs				
Capital Costs				
new construction				
retrofitting existing facilities				
major repairs				
equipment				
other 1				
other 2				
other 3				
Total Capital Costs				
Total All Costs				
Cost Estimate from Template 14				
Difference				
Incremental Operating Revenue				
Program Revenue				
fees				
sales				
other 1				
other 2				
other 3				

	Goal 1A	Goal 1B	Goal 1C	Total All Goals
Earned Income				
admissions				
memberships				
facilities rental fees				
sales				
other 1				
other 2				
other 3				
Raised Revenue				
grants				
gifts				
sponsorships				
other 1				
other 2				
other 3				
Investment Income				
draw on designated funds				
Total Operating Revenue				
Capital Funds				
grants				
gifts				
designated campaign				
other				
Total Capital Revenue				
Net Operating Revenue				
Net Capital Revenue				

is positive, the projections in the detailed budgets exceed the planning estimates. Negative numbers indicate a potential budget surplus. In either case, these differences may reflect staff members' more realistic and complete knowledge of specific operational costs.

There are several ways to bring costs into alignment. If there is a surplus in one budget category, it can be applied to another where there is a shortfall. Sometimes resources may be diverted from existing programs and projects, reducing the need for new funding. Funds may be freed up by eliminating programs that are no longer successful, finding ways to cut expenses, or working more efficiently. For example, funds in the museum's publications budget might be moved from a quarterly e-zine to new gallery guides. More effective use of volunteers, such as training docents to deliver after-school workshops, can reduce staff costs associated with expanding such programs. Joining a purchasing cooperative might bring down the cost of acid-free storage materials, helping to fund an assessment by a conservator. All of these examples assume shifting funds within specific departments. Taking a broader perspective would involve reallocating funds across all departments, not just within a single department.

If the two sets of numbers continue to be significantly out of alignment, staff should go back to the budget task force with recommended revisions. The task force will return to **Template 14: Operating Plan Worksheets** to adjust the estimated expenses for individual goals, reallocating funds to bring the total budget for all goals into line with the task force's initial estimates or revising the estimated cost of the plan. If the changes are significant, the task force may need to go back to the entire Strategic Planning Team to think creatively about alternative objectives. It may also be helpful to alert the board and seek its guidance in prioritizing initiatives, goals, and objectives.

PROJECTING REVENUES

The lower half of the spreadsheets in **Template 15: Cost and Revenue Worksheets** determines how the museum will cover the projected costs. The sources of revenue include the following:

- *Program revenues* are associated with specific programs such as admission fees for a temporary exhibition, proceeds from catalog sales, dedicated gifts and grants, or enrollment fees for classes.
- *Earned income* is generated by the museum's own operations, such as membership and restaurant revenues, some of which may support a particular initiative. For example, if the initiative calls for boosting membership from particular target audiences, increased membership fees can help defray the costs.
- *Raised revenues* are those that flow to the museum from outside sources. This category might include gifts, in-kind contributions, and general fundraising.
- *Investment income* includes allocations from designated funds that may be spent on particular initiatives.
- *Capital funds* are earmarked for expenses such as facilities improvements and other major projects in the budget.

The task force and staff will undoubtedly encounter situations in which it is not possible to cover the costs associated with particular strategic initiatives using readily identifiable revenue sources. Funding shortfalls call for creative thinking to determine how additional revenues might be generated or how anticipated costs might be reduced. Are program fees comparable to other programs in the region, or could they be raised? Is there a potential donor or corporate sponsor who has a particular interest in this initiative or audience?

In essence, the staff is being asked to determine whether all of the strategic goals and objectives are financially feasible. Will one or more need to be reduced in scope? Will they need to be phased in over the multiyear planning period? Since Template 15 involves more detailed thinking within the broad parameters set by the task force, it may be necessary to revisit Template 14 to make adjustments. Strategic thinking is an ongoing, iterative process that sometimes requires retracing steps in order to move forward.

PROJECTING OVER THE LIFE OF THE PLAN

In **Template 11B: Goals and Objectives Worksheet**, the Strategic Planning Team sketched out the sequence of plan objectives by assigning them a time frame. Staff members will use this template to review those projections, determining annual costs and revenue and fine-tuning the plan and budget.

Template 16: Multiyear Budget Worksheets is linked to the other Excel workbooks; the total budget estimates for each strategic initiative will be transferred to these spreadsheets. There is a page for each initiative, with room for multiple years of budget projections. There is also a summary spreadsheet where the costs and revenue for all initiatives are summarized by year.

TEMPLATE 16: MULTIYEAR BUDGET WORKSHEETS

Strategic Initiative						
	Year 1	Year 2	Year 3	Total All Years	Template 15 Estimates	Variance
Incremental Operating Costs						
additional, new staff						
contractors, consultants						
technology hardware and software						
materials development, design, and printing						
marketing						
research						
evaluation						
supplies						
exhibition or facilities design and construction						
maintenance contracts						
training and professional development						
fundraising						
equipment						
other 1						
other 2						
other 3						
other 4						
Total Operating Costs						
Capital Costs						
new construction						
retrofitting existing facilities						
major repairs						
equipment						
other 1						
other 2						
other 3						
Total Capital Costs						
Total All Costs						

Incremental Operating Revenue

	Year 1	Year 2	Year 3	Total All Years	Template 15 Estimates	Variance
Program Revenue						
fees						
sales						
other 1						
other 2						
other 3						
Earned Income						
admissions						
memberships						
facilities rental fees						
sales						
other 1						
other 2						
other 3						
Raised Revenue						
grants						
gifts						
sponsorships						
other 1						
other 2						
other 3						
Investment Income						
draw on designated funds						
Total Operating Revenue						
Capital Funds						
grants						
gifts						
designated campaign						
other						
Total Capital Revenue						
Net Operating Revenue						
Net Capital Revenue						

Because of the complexity of projecting costs and revenues of multiple goals per initiative over multiple years, there is no template that captures all of the considerations. Staff may need to develop multiyear budgets for particular goals on working spreadsheets, transferring the totals to Template 16.

As staff members think about the timing and sequencing of the objectives in the plan, they need to consider several factors. Limits on staff capacity, finances, and facilities make it impossible for the museum to take on every piece of the plan in the first year. Some objectives may be predicated on accomplishing other objectives, which set the stage for later work. Objectives often span traditional departmental lines, which requires coordination and proactive planning. For example, implementing a new docent training program may be most strategic after reinstallation plans for the permanent collection are completed but before the galleries are installed. The work of sequencing objectives and preparing year-by-year budgets should, therefore, be done by either a cross-functional team or a senior manager who has a broad perspective on the work of the entire staff.

Once again, the projections have to be tested against the reality of financial resources. If **Template 15: Cost and Revenue Worksheets** produces balanced budgets, there is still a question of timing. Many factors need to be taken into account in finalizing the sequencing of objectives and related expenses. For example, costs are often incurred ahead of any earned revenue, potentially creating a cash-flow problem. It may take months or years to successfully secure large project grants. The development department may need to stretch fundraising efforts over several years to avoid donor fatigue. As the Strategic Planning Team and senior management consider the multiyear budgets, they will inevitably adjust the timing of the plan. Larger, more expensive projects may need to be scheduled later in the plan to ensure that there are adequate funds. Then again, projects that may have originally been anticipated to take place toward the end of the planning period may attract funding sooner than expected. Because this is an iterative process, it needs to be reviewed at least quarterly.

The detailed cost and revenue estimates from Template 14 are automatically transferred to each strategic initiative worksheet of Template 15, ensuring that the year-by-year budgets remain in line with the projections. If the "Variance to Estimate" figure is positive, the detailed estimates exceed the amount budgeted. If the differences are significant, the costs and revenue should be reviewed again. If the variance is a negative number, the detailed costs are lower than projections—always good news!

TAKE NOTE!
- The three templates in this chapter accommodate five initiatives, each of which has space for five goals. This number should be adequate for most plans. If the plan has fewer initiatives, goals, or objectives, the administrator can simply delete appropriate rows, columns, or entire worksheets. However, it is critical that the names of the workbooks and individual sheets are not changed or the links between the sheets will be broken. Adding lines or sheets is somewhat more difficult because the links rely on named cells, which cannot simply be copied and pasted. Expanding the sheets and workbook to accommodate additional initiatives or goals can be done by someone who understands that feature in Excel and patiently replicates the series of links between the spreadsheets.
- There are links that automatically move information from Templates 11A, 11B, and 12 to Templates 13, 14, and 15 and between the three budget templates. Those cells are shaded light gray.
- In Template 16, planners may prefer to change the headers on the year-by-year columns from "year 1," "year 2," and so on to the relevant fiscal years. This will require many changes but can be done using the Replace feature in Excel.

7

Phase 7

Report and Monitor

Most board members are familiar with voluminous planning documents that end up gathering dust on a bookshelf. They may have even experienced the frustration of investing time and energy in a well-intended planning process and seeing the fruits of their labor buried in the sheer volume of daily obligations and operational detail. This is likely to happen when strategic planning is viewed as a self-contained, time-limited exercise. But as part of the ongoing process of strategic thinking, it should be woven into the fabric of institutional life at all levels.

In this phase, members of the Strategic Planning Team will write a document that communicates the spirit and intent of the plan to stakeholders. Then a task force, staff, and board members will work together to build strategic thinking and planning into ongoing operations. Led by the director, the staff will report progress on a regular basis, and the board will monitor ongoing performance against the plan. This step may seem like an obvious part of the planning process; however, *Museum Board Leadership 2017* reports that only 52 percent of museum boards regularly monitor the organization's progress against strategic plan goals.[1] Planning without monitoring results (and modifying the plan when necessary) has no long-term value.

Two templates will measure the impact of the efforts of the board, staff, volunteers, and other stakeholders:

- **Template 17: Operating Plan Report** generates regular reports on the status of strategic initiatives and goals. It should be presented and discussed at board meetings every three to six months or whenever there is a particular milestone in the realization of the plan.
- **Template 18: Strategic Plan Update** is a PowerPoint presentation that gives the board and staff a big-picture overview of how activities have come together in realizing the museum's strategic plan. This update should be the focus of special board and staff presentations each year.

THE STRATEGIC PLAN IS MORE THAN A DOCUMENT

The plan is far more than a summary of institutional goals that is filed away and dusted off periodically: it is the outcome of rigorous and creative thinking about the future of the museum. While the process of strategic thinking is ongoing, it is now time to piece together the varied elements that have surfaced in the Strategic Planning Team's discussions and share them with others. We do not offer a template for this document because there is no preferred format. As in quilt making, the pieces can be assembled in many different ways, depending on the purpose and intended audience.

Up to this point the focus has been on the skills of strategic thinking and the process of strategic planning rather than the task of writing a strategic plan document. This approach has been intentional, because too often planning ends up focusing on the final document as the result of the process rather than as a tool for communicating highlights of the plan to others. The document itself is indeed important; in fact, many will refer to it as the "Strategic Plan." For those who haven't served on the Strategic Planning Team, it serves a critical function. It guides board members, staff members, volunteers, and other museum stakeholders in achieving the goals and objectives defined in the planning process.

THE INFORMATION NEEDED TO CREATE THE PLANNING DOCUMENT

In effect, the Strategic Planning Team has been writing the plan in the course of articulating the museum's mission, vision, and values statements; identifying strategic initiatives, goals, and objectives; and creating mechanisms that link them to the budget. Now it is a matter of organizing these components into a single, coherent, and compelling document. Retracing the phases of the team's work and extracting the key elements captured through the templates and other exercises can literally lead to assembling the "strategic plan." The administrator or the person who facilitated the planning process should assemble, at minimum, the following work products:

- Mission statements—both the new and the previous versions to show the evolution of thinking
- Vision statement and other supporting documents
- **Template 11A: Strategic Initiatives Worksheet**
- **Template 11B: Goals and Objectives Worksheet**
- **Template 14: Operating Plan Worksheets**
- **Template 15: Cost and Revenue Worksheets**

Expressed in these documents and templates are the key decisions about institutional mission, goals, and objectives as well as estimates of the costs and associated revenues required to achieve them. Taken together, these components are the strategic plan.

Consider taking a modular approach to assembling the document. At its core is the framework of the plan, which can be augmented by additional components to create documents of different lengths for different purposes and audiences. At one end of the spectrum would be a brief executive summary with the mission statement and highlights of the plan, which would be of interest to the public and funding agencies. At the other would be a detailed operational plan including financial projections and performance measures, which would provide a record of the team's deliberations and guidelines for the board, staff, and other stakeholders charged with implementing and monitoring the plan.

To make the plan document meaningful and readable, the writers will need to

- choose the material that is most important to particular readers
- decide the order that best communicates the priorities of the plan
- find a length that is concise but thorough
- provide enough detail so that board, staff, and other internal stakeholders can use it as a guide
- select a tone that conveys the spirit of the process
- present a distillation of the process that captures the thinking that went into making decisions and setting priorities
- stress the institution-wide nature of the plan

Since the plan was conceived cross-departmentally, the document should be written in a way that shows integration of roles and responsibilities rather than the silos that sometimes exist, particularly in large institutions. It should be optimistic, yet realistic, inspiring internal and external stakeholders to maximize the museum's potential.

WRITE FOR THE RIGHT AUDIENCE

Because the planning document is a communications tool, it is essential to keep the image of its readers and users in mind as components are written and assembled. In a typical museum, the primary audiences will be the board, staff, and funders. In museums that are arms of city, county, or state government, readers will also include city council members or state legislators. In university museums, the document should be geared toward deans and other members of the administration.

From conception to final draft, focus on the priorities of those who will be reading the document. If, for example, the museum is governed by a founding board that is deeply committed to underlying mission and values, give these elements a prominent position in the document. If, however, the museum is governed by a board of mayoral appointees who are grappling with budget cuts, be sure to emphasize how the plan makes the most of diminishing financial resources.

Whoever the audience, the language should be lively and engaging, free from jargon or insider vocabulary. It should aim to be more like a good magazine story than an academic paper. It should be easy to follow, with clear organization and structure.

HOW TO USE THE DOCUMENT

The primary purpose of the document is to guide board, staff, and other internal stakeholders in realizing the goals articulated in the plan. It will also serve a variety of purposes for external stakeholders such as the following:

- *Museum website.* The mission, vision, and values statements should be easy to find on the museum's website. A summary version of the strategic plan document should also be readily accessible as a downloadable document from the "About" page. Incorporating photos and other illustrations can help to convey the breadth of the museum's collections and activities, as well as the communities served.
- *Newsletter articles and blog posts.* The strategic plan can generate an interesting series of articles or blogs, each focusing on a strategic initiative and reporting on progress to date. The strategic planning process itself and the perspectives of individual participants could also lead to a rich feature story that provides a behind-the-scenes look at museum planning.
- *Fundraising case statements.* The strategic plan document will be useful in all types of fundraising, from capital campaigns to grant requests. Those initiatives that require funding can be highlighted and linked to strategic goals and initiatives to establish their importance to the future of the institution.
- *Annual reports.* The new mission statement should be featured prominently, followed by an acknowledgment of the Strategic Planning Team's significant contributions of time and energy. The executive summary provides a good overview for members and other readers. It may be supplemented by financial reports, especially as the initiatives set forth in the strategic plan relate to the annual budget.
- *Targeted mailings to key constituencies.* Initiatives that address the needs of particular communities can be selected and used to build audiences and demonstrate the museum's commitment to providing public value.
- *Advertising and promotional materials.* The mission statement, supporting documents, and photographs of Strategic Planning Team members can be used in a variety of ways to support the museum's marketing and fund development goals.

ELEMENTS TO INCLUDE IN THE PLANNING DOCUMENT

The following components can be arranged—and rearranged—in whatever order will be most meaningful to particular readers:

- *Letter of introduction from the director or board chair.* This letter should show support for the vision of the museum's future. It may also explain how the process was initiated and acknowledge the Strategic Planning Team to establish the level of stakeholder involvement and commitment.
- *Executive summary outlining the main points of the plan.* This section should provide a concise and compelling sense of the plan and its potential for those who are interested but not integrally involved with the museum. One to two pages is an ideal length.
- *Roster of Strategic Planning Team members with their affiliations and contributions.* Here is the place to thank them publicly and identify them as the authors of the plan.
- *Mission statement.* As the foundational document on which the plan is built, this should be featured clearly and prominently. It may be followed by an explanation or discussion of how it was crafted or modified, but the statement itself should stand alone.
- *Vision and values statements that augment the mission statement.* They can simply be stated without discussion.
- *Overview of the planning process, including the methodology of the environmental scan.* This section is an opportunity to demonstrate the broadly participatory nature of the process and the thinking and deliberations that informed the plan, including emerging trends in the field. Capturing the rationale underlying the specific recommendations in the plan will help the board and staff to see the planning process as a touchstone as circumstances and opportunities change.
- *Key strategic issues that must be addressed for the museum to advance its mission and vision and the goals and objectives that support each strategic issue.* This information should be presented in a concise format that moves from the general to the specific.
- *Operational plan that links the strategic initiatives, goals, and objectives to responsibilities, resources, and time frames.*
- *Performance monitors to show how success will be measured by staff and board members.* These may be described in general terms or illustrated through examples of the actual tools and benchmarks.
- *Organizational history and profile to provide a context for the museum and establish a starting point for the new plan.* This section gives readers who may be unfamiliar with the institution a brief record of its recent history and current status.
- *Appendices.* These may include a summary of the Strategic Planning Team survey results, a summary of research undertaken during the environmental scan including the names and affiliations of community members who participated, the final SWOT analysis, an organizational chart, staff and board rosters, a projected financial statement, budget reports for previous years, and data on attendance, membership, and community support. This material can be provided in the form of spreadsheets, tables, or graphic displays.

Some museums elect to keep portions of the work of the Strategic Planning Team confidential or separate from the planning documents. These may include detailed budgets, long-term staffing plans, programmatic assessments, plans for work that is more operational than strategic, and findings that reveal the museum's shortcomings. While the latter may not be reported to the public, it is essential that they be addressed with an action plan, the progress of which is monitored.

Case in point: One museum concluded that the composition of the board was a significant problem. It was very small, with little turnover, and not broadly representative of the community. In short, it lacked the skills required to govern a twenty-first-century institution. When a draft of the plan was shared with a local funder, she responded, "Never give me a plan that says you need to 'rebuild the board.' I won't fund an organization that does not have a strong board."

WRITING THE PLANNING DOCUMENT

"In our case it was inevitable that I would take the lead in writing the document," says the director of a museum with a staff of ten. Working hand in hand with a consultant, the director had orchestrated the planning process and served as the liaison with internal and external stakeholders. Within larger organizational structures, the assistant director or associate director might take a lead role in writing the draft with the director doing substantial editing before sending it to the rest of the team for review.

If a consultant has facilitated the planning process, they will continue to serve as an advisor during this phase of the work. In the same way that they guided the conversations in Strategic Planning Team meetings without doing most of the talking, they have a role to play in helping to shape the planning document. Some consultants will include writing the planning documents as part of their services, with staff and board acting as contributors and editors. Others will swap those roles, with staff members doing the writing and the consultant editing their work. Let there be no doubt: this is the museum's plan for its future, not the consultant's plan for the museum. The writing and editing must be a collaborative effort.

GETTING FEEDBACK AND APPROVAL

The draft will generally have one principal author who works closely with a collaborator or two. They will exchange and refine early drafts until they arrive at a version that covers all the bases. At that point, the draft will be circulated to all members of the Strategic Planning Team, giving them ample time to review the document. Many museums elect to reconvene the Strategic Planning Team for this final review. Consider their comments and incorporate them, as appropriate, in a final draft, which is then sent to the board for its approval. This vitally important document calls for more than a rubber stamp, so schedule adequate time for dialogue at a board meeting. After incorporating the board's comments in a final draft, the document will benefit from professional editing, either by an in-house staff member or by a freelance editor. Only then is the document ready to be shared with external stakeholders.

With the strategic planning document completed and distributed, there may be a tendency to think that the work of strategic thinking is completed, but concerted effort must continue if the plan is to be realized. In truth, the strategic thought process has entered a new monitoring phase in which performance is continually viewed in light of the plan.

OVERSEEING IMPLEMENTATION OF THE PLAN

Effective implementation of the strategic plan is so important to long-term institutional success that the director and the board must retain ultimate oversight. But given their many other responsibilities, it is helpful from a practical perspective to designate a person or group that is responsible for staying on top of the plan's many facets on an ongoing basis. This group might be a Strategy Committee of the board, augmented by key staff members, or a designated ad hoc team (perhaps including members of the Strategic Planning Team). Smaller task forces may also be organized around each strategic initiative to report to one of these groups. Whatever team is selected will be responsible for completing **Template 17: Operating Plan Report** and **Template 18: Strategic Plan Update**, presenting them to the board and answering any questions that may arise.

MAKING BOARD MEETINGS MORE STRATEGIC

Board meetings filled with reports from standing committees that result in excursions into pressing but not necessarily strategic issues lead to a preoccupation with operational details and allow the board to drift away from the practice of strategic thinking. To make the best use of board members' time and talents, typical board agendas can be replaced with strategic agendas. This shift makes perfect sense after the adoption of a new strategic plan. It will set the tone for strategic thinking and create a sense of momentum and teamwork toward a common goal.

Thomas McLaughlin describes the advantages of a strategic agenda, organized around the initiatives and goals of the plan: "It creates a sense of momentum and teamwork toward a common goal. The goals board members worked so hard to identify during their strategic planning retreat show up exactly as crafted on every board meeting agenda. Members know that they will be able to engage in the dialogue, and the back-and-forth nature of committee material makes it easier for them to engage in the discussion because there won't be long stretches of time when they are expected to be passive listeners."[2]

Instead of relying on reports from "standing committees"—which, in the words of one board consultant, are aptly named—encourage forward thinking by appointing task forces to monitor the progress on specific strategic initiatives. Another option is to identify committees whose functions relate to aspects of the strategic goals, charging them to report on feedback from internal and external stakeholders. For example, the Finance Committee might conduct an analysis of the profitability of a new initiative, or the Program Committee might document the need for a new outreach program. There are several advantages to this approach:

- It makes board meetings more meaningful and keeps trustees' attention.
- It replaces the inherently backward-looking nature of regular reports with future-oriented discussions.
- It keeps strategic issues and goals in the forefront of board members' minds.
- It makes clear the connection between board agendas and the museum's purpose.

Another way to monitor overall institutional performance is to distribute an updated dashboard ahead of every meeting. A brief memo annotating significant data on the dashboard will help board members focus on key indicators and progress toward goals.

In addition to regular review of performance and progress toward agreed-upon benchmarks, agendas should include in-depth discussions of one or more strategic initiatives at each meeting. Background materials should be distributed in advance of the meeting so that members are ready to engage in substantive dialogue about emerging issues and trends. This approach enables the board to break out of the kind of informal reporting and meandering conversations that can leave strategic issues off the table.

The Strategic Planning Team may remain in place with responsibility for monitoring progress and making adjustments to the plan. Alternatively, a new ad hoc strategy task force or the Executive Committee may be assigned responsibility. That group should schedule the sequence of reports and meetings to coincide with institutional and board calendars, taking into account activities, events, and other reports that may inform deliberations. For example, discussion of a strategic initiative related to sustainability might be scheduled after the results of the annual appeal and major fundraising events are in hand. Table 7.1 is a calendar for a community historical society whose plan includes three strategic initiatives and whose board meets every other month.

Table 7.1

Month	Society Activities	Board Activities	Plan Review
September	• School tours begin	• Annual meeting and elections of members and officers • Finalize composition of board committees	• Dashboard report • Operating plan report
October	• Harvest Festival	• Orientation for new board members • Board committees set work plans and meeting schedules	
November	• Close and de-install annual exhibition	• Board meeting	• In-depth discussion of Initiative 2: Expand the circle of participation and support, grounded in the society's commitment to serving the entire community • Dashboard report • Operating plan report
December	• Annual appeal letters • Holiday open house		
January	• Historic properties close • Annual winter symposium	• Board meeting • Receive audit	• In-depth discussion of Initiative 3: Ensure that the society has the capacity and resources to continue its role as steward of the community's history and our treasured historic properties • Dashboard report • Operating plan report
February	• Clean and inventory collections storage		
March	• Finalize gala plans; select and secure honorees	• Board meeting • Set priorities for board recruitment	• In-depth discussion of Initiative 1: Document and share the stories of the community's history in ways that are inclusive, accessible, and meaningful to a wide range of residents and visitors to the community • Dashboard report
April	• Gala • Install annual exhibition	• Governance Committee meetings re: nominations	
May	• Reopen historic properties	• Annual board retreat	• Annual plan review
June		• Finance Committee begins budget process	
July		• Board meeting • Accept next FY budget	• Dashboard report • Operating plan report
August	• Recruit and train school tour leaders		

MONITORING DETAILS OF IMPLEMENTING THE STRATEGIC PLAN

While the board must guard against any urge to micromanage, it has a responsibility to know that operational details, especially those that relate to achieving strategic goals, are being handled effectively. **Template 17: Operating Plan Report** is an Excel workbook with a worksheet for each strategic initiative. Each worksheet lists the goals and objectives supporting the initiative, along with the status of programs and activities. The time frame established for each objective in **Template 11B: Goals and Objectives Worksheet** is entered automatically, along with the individual or group responsible. In the final column, staff enters a status update. Primarily a management tool, this update also gives the board a snapshot of how things are progressing.

TEMPLATE 17: OPERATING PLAN REPORT

Strategic Initiative 1
Integrate the museum into academics, research, and student life on campus

Green: On track
Yellow: Caution
Red: Serious issues

Goals	Objectives	Responsibility	Time Frame	Status	
A. Increase curricular connections with a broad spectrum of academic departments	1. Establish an academic advisory board	Director of academic programs; chair of natural sciences dept.	Fall semester 2018	First meeting Nov. 2018; board has continued to meet every semester. Added reps from English and history depts. Fall 2019.	green
	2. Provide mini-grants to faculty to develop new ways to use the museum for teaching classes	Director of academic programs; academic advisory board	2019–2020 and 2020–2021 academic years	First grant cycle delayed to spring 2020; one grant made spring 2020 and fall 2020. Two grants awarded spring 2021, which meets the 2 grants/semester goal.	was yellow on last report, now green
	3. Strategize with administration about the role the museum can play in university efforts to recruit science majors	Executive director; director of marketing	Spring semester 2019	Admissions office cancelled several meetings to discuss this. No time allotted for reception during accepted students weekend.	red: there does not appear to be support for this objective. DROP?

KEEPING THE BIG PICTURE IN FOCUS

Once or twice a year, the board and staff should receive a more formal presentation of the overall status of the implementation of the strategic plan. **Template 18: Strategic Plan Update** is a PowerPoint presentation to use at a retreat or special focus meeting. To make this presentation more engaging, print and distribute "Notes Page" versions of each slide with materials that report key indicators of institutional performance, such as the dashboard reports described in Phase 5.

The slides in this presentation are the most generic format: white slides with san serif type. Customize the design to include your museum's logo, color scheme, and typeface. Create an agenda on slide 2, substituting your strategic initiatives for the placeholder text. The mission and vision statements developed in Phase 2 are fundamental to the

TEMPLATE 18: STRATEGIC PLAN UPDATE

[Museum Name]

Strategic Plan Update
[date]

Type Your Museum's Name Here

Agenda

- Strategy Update
  - Strategic Initiative 1
  - Strategic Initiative 2
  - Strategic Initiative 3
  - Strategic Initiative 4
  - Strategic Initiative 5
- Summary
  - Progress to date
  - Issues to be addressed

Type Your Museum's Name Here

[Museum name]

- Mission statement

Type Your Museum's Name Here

[Museum name]

- Vision

Type Your Museum's Name Here

[Strategic Initiative 1]

[Goal A]
- [each objective and status – on track, delayed or jeopardized]

Type Your Museum's Name Here

[Strategic Initiative 1]

[Goal B]
- [each objective and status – on track, delayed or jeopardized]

Type Your Museum's Name Here

[Strategic Initiative 2]

[Goal A]
- [each objective and status – on track, delayed or jeopardized]

Type Your Museum's Name Here

[Strategic Initiative 3]

[Goal A]
- [each objective and status – on track, delayed or jeopardized]

Type Your Museum's Name Here

[Strategic Initiative 4]

[Goal A]
- [each objective and status – on track, delayed or jeopardized]

Type Your Museum's Name Here

[Strategic Initiative 5]

[Goal A]
- [each objective and status – on track, delayed or jeopardized]

Type Your Museum's Name Here

Summary

Progress to date
- In a series of bullets, summarize major accomplishments since the last update
- How is the museum doing in terms of progress on strategic initiatives?
- What evidence is there of progress?

Type Your Museum's Name Here

Summary

Issues to be addressed
- In a series of bullets, summarize any difficulties or issues
- How significant or urgent are these issues?
- Can the board help to resolve these issues?
- Do Goals or Objectives need to be modified?
- Do Strategic Initiatives need to be revisited?

Type Your Museum's Name Here

whole strategic thinking exercise. Insert them on slides 3 and 4 to keep them in the forefront of board members' minds. On the following slides, add each strategic initiative, along with the relevant goals and objectives, inserting additional slides as needed. Indicate whether the objective is on track for completion within the established time frame, encountering some delay or difficulty that requires closer monitoring, or encountering problems that may jeopardize reaching the objective. Color coding the comments with green (on track), yellow (caution), or red (alert) highlights or bullets will help the board identify areas of concern. A brief explanation should be inserted next to any objectives that are not on track.

On the final slides, consider all initiatives and summarize where the institution stands in terms of implementing its strategic plan. Focusing on progress to date, the next-to-last slide calls for bullet points that summarize the major achievements since the last update. Questions to be answered are:

- How is the museum doing in terms of achieving its strategic initiatives?
- What specific evidence is there that progress is being made?

The final slide allows the implementation team to note any significant concerns, environmental trends, internal changes, or problems that may require some modification in the plan. Another series of bullet points summarizes where issues have arisen that must be addressed in order to realize strategic initiatives. Questions to be answered here include:

- How significant and/or urgent are these issues in terms of affecting the achievement of strategic initiatives?
- Are there issues or problems the board can help resolve? How?
- What modifications might be required to the goals or objectives?

MODIFYING THE PLAN

In reviewing the progress that has been made and the challenges that remain, it may become apparent to the board and staff that certain changes need to be considered. Strategic thinking often calls for revisions to existing plans. As noted earlier, a well-articulated mission and vision will not only allow revisions but also suggest what changes are needed. In keeping with their respective areas of responsibility, the board should outline its general concerns, leaving it to the staff to suggest the specific changes that will address these concerns. If a particular objective is not proving viable, it may need to be revised or deleted. If a particular goal is not being advanced by the objectives outlined in the plan, it may be appropriate to create new objectives. A goal may even be modified to better support a strategic initiative. However, because of the centrality of strategic initiatives, they should only be reconsidered and potentially revised by the full board when circumstances have changed dramatically. If modifications to goals and/or objectives are called for, edit Templates 11A and 11B. Those changes will then be reflected in all of the subsequent templates.

CONCLUDING BY COMING FULL CIRCLE

With each Strategic Plan Update, the strategic thinking and planning process comes full circle. The ongoing monitoring will continue to reveal ways in which the strategy can be refined and the museum can more effectively meet its strategic goals and fulfill its mission. In short, it will lead to systemic change. By the time the next formal planning exercise rolls around, the board, the director, and the senior staff—indeed, all internal stakeholders—will have adopted new ways of thinking, planning, and, most important, acting strategically.

NOTES

1. BoardSource, *Museum Board Leadership 2017: A National Report* (Washington, DC: BoardSource, 2017), 21.

2. Thomas A. McLaughlin, "The Strategic Board Agenda," accessed February 15, 2018, https://www.compasspoint.org/board-cafe/strategic-board-agenda.

Resource Guide for *Strategic Thinking and Planning*

PUBLICATIONS

Allison, Michael, and Jude Kaye. *Strategic Planning for Nonprofit Organizations: A Practical Guide for Dynamic Times*. New York: John Wiley & Sons, 2015.

Allison, Mike. "In Defense of Strategic Planning: A Rebuttal." Blue Avocado blog post accessed March 12, 2018. San Francisco: CompassPoint (now American Nonprofits).

Anderson, Gail, ed. *Museum Mission Statements: Building a Distinct Identity*. Washington, DC: American Association of Museums, 1998.

Barry, Bryan W. *Strategic Planning Workbook for Nonprofit Organizations*. St. Paul, MN: Amherst H. Wilder Foundation, 1997.

BoardSource. *Strategic Planning Understanding the Process: A BoardSource Toolkit*. Washington, DC: BoardSource, 2011.

Bryson, John M. *Strategic Planning for Public and Nonprofit Organizations: A Guide to Strengthening and Sustaining Organizational Achievement*. San Francisco: Jossey-Bass, 2018.

Butler, Lawrence. *The Nonprofit Dashboard: Using Metrics to Drive Mission Success*. Washington, DC: BoardSource, 2012.

Drucker, Peter. *The Drucker Foundation Self-Assessment Tool*. New York and San Francisco: Drucker Foundation and Jossey-Bass, 1999.

Grace, Kay Sprinkle, John A. Yankey, and Amy McClellan. *The Nonprofit Board's Role in Mission, Planning and Evaluation*. Washington, DC: BoardSource, 2008.

Jackson, Peter M. "Performance Indicators: Promises and Pitfalls." In *Museum Economics and the Community*, ed. Susan M. Pearce. London: Athlone Press, 2000.

Jacobsen, John W. *Measuring Museum Impact and Performance*. Lanham, MD: Rowman & Littlefield, 2016.

Jacobsen, John, Victor Becker, Duane Kocik, and Jeannie Stahl. *The Museum Manager's Compendium: 101 Essential Tools and Resources*. Lanham, MD: Rowman & Littlefield, 2017.

La Piana, David. *The Nonprofit Strategy Revolution: Real-Time Strategic Planning in a Rapid-Response World*. New York: Fieldstone Alliance, 2008.

Light, Mark. *The Strategic Board: The Step-by-Step Guide to High-Impact Governance*. New York: John Wiley & Sons, 2001.

Lord, Gail Dexter, and Kate Markert. *The Manual of Strategic Planning for Cultural Organizations: A Guide for Museums, Performing Arts, Science Centers, Public Gardens, Heritage Sites, Libraries, Archives and Zoos.* Lanham, MD: Rowman & Littlefield, 2017.

McNamara, Carter. *Field Guide to Nonprofit Strategic Planning and Facilitation.* Minneapolis, MN: Authenticity Consulting, 2007. (See also Mr. McNamara's online management library at https://managementhelp.org/strategicplanning/index.htm.)

"Mission Accomplished: The Board's Role in Outcome Measurement." *Board Member* 10, no. 8 (September 2001).

Mittenthal, Richard A. "Ten Keys to Successful Strategic Planning for Nonprofit and Foundation Leaders." Briefing Paper. New York: TCC Group, 2002.

"Strategic Planning: Design for the Future." *Board Member* 11, no. 5 (May 2002).

"Tapping into the Board's Talents." *Board Member* 17, no. 5 (September/October 2008): 8–11.

Waechter, Susan A. *Driving Strategic Planning: A Nonprofit Executive's Guide.* Washington, DC: BoardSource, 2010.

ORGANIZATIONS

Alliance for Nonprofit Management
www.allianceonline.org

American Nonprofits
www.americannonprofits.org

BoardSource
https://boardsource.org

CompassPoint Nonprofit Services
https://www.compasspoint.org

National Council of Nonprofits
https://www.councilofnonprofits.org/tools-resources/strategic-planning-nonprofits

Appendix

Mission, Vision, and Values Statements

MISSION

These mission statements meet most of the tests of compelling and useful missions.

San Diego Museum of Man, San Diego, California
Inspiring human connections by exploring the human experience.

National Building Museum, Washington, DC
Our mission is to advance the quality of the built environment by educating people about its impact on their lives.

State Historical Society of Iowa, Des Moines, Iowa
We empower Iowa to build and sustain culturally vibrant communities by connecting Iowans to the people, places, and points of pride that define our state.

Museum of International Folk Art, Santa Fe, New Mexico
The mission of the Museum of International Folk Art is to foster understanding of the traditional arts to illuminate human creativity and shape a humane world.

Oakland Museum of California, Oakland, California
The mission of the Oakland Museum of California is to inspire all Californians to create a more vibrant future for themselves and their communities.

Children's Museum of the Arts, New York, New York
The mission of the Children's Museum of the Arts is to introduce children and their families to the transformative power of the arts by providing opportunities to make art side by side with working artists.

Franklin Institute, Philadelphia, Pennsylvania
In the spirit of inquiry and discovery embodied by Benjamin Franklin, the mission of The Franklin Institute is to inspire a passion for learning about science and technology.

University of Michigan Museum of Art, Ann Arbor, Michigan
The University of Michigan Museum of Art seeks to transform individual and civic life by promoting the discovery, contemplation, and enjoyment of the art of our world.

National Zoo, Washington, DC
At the Smithsonian's National Zoo and Conservation Biology Institute, we save species. We provide engaging experiences with animals and create and share knowledge to save wildlife and habitats.

Woodland Park Zoo, Seattle, Washington
Woodland Park Zoo saves animals and their habitats through conservation leadership and engaging experiences, inspiring people to learn, care, and act.

VISION

The following vision statements express changes the museums seek to achieve in their communities and the larger world. Comparing mission and vision statements illustrates how the two are different.

Brooklyn Museum, Brooklyn, New York
Our mission: To create inspiring encounters with art that expand the ways we see ourselves, the world, and its possibilities.
Our vision: Where great art and courageous conversations are catalysts for a more connected, civic, and empathetic world.

Shedd Aquarium, Chicago, Illinois
Our mission: Sparking compassion, curiosity, and conservation for the aquatic animal world.
Our vision: A world thriving with aquatic life, sustained by people who love, understand, and protect it.

The Anacostia Community Museum, Washington, DC
The mission is to enhance understanding of contemporary urban experiences and strengthen community bonds by conserving the past, documenting the present, and serving as a catalyst for shaping the future.
Our vision of the Smithsonian's Anacostia Community Museum is to challenge perceptions, generate new knowledge, and deepen understanding about the ever-changing concepts and realities of communities.

Museum of Art and History, Santa Cruz, California
Our mission is to ignite shared experiences and unexpected connections. We accomplish this mission when we bring people together around art and history through dynamic exhibitions, events, partnerships, and programs.
When we are successful, our work helps build a stronger, more connected community. That's the impact that we seek.

Detroit Institute of Art, Detroit, Michigan
Mission: The DIA creates experiences that help each visitor find personal meaning in art, individually and with each other.
Vision: The DIA will be the town square of our community, a gathering place for everybody.

The Tech, San Jose, California

Our mission: To inspire the innovator in everyone.

Our vision: The Tech, by what it does directly and through others, helps build a civil society that enables everyone, especially low-income young people, to succeed in a world driven by technology.

VALUES

There are many ways to express a museum's values, core beliefs, or operating principles. These examples capture the unique spirit and commitments of these museums.

Boston Children's Museum, Boston, Massachusetts

We believe in the intrinsic value of play and provide opportunities for experiential learning and multisensory, object-based exploration.

We connect children and families to transformational experiences and ideas in science and technology, health and wellness, arts and humanities, and global cultures.

We support parents, caregivers, educators, scientific researchers, civic leaders, and health professionals in addressing critical issues facing children.

We embrace change and innovation in order to address the changing landscape of childhood.

We introduce children and families to the diverse cultural life of the city and are a vibrant urban meeting place for all in Boston and beyond.

The Tech, San Jose, California

Our Values: Tech, Yeah!

We say YES to PEOPLE

We recognize the unique value and creative potential in everyone. Through programs, exhibits, and events we commit to honor and support this potential by inspiring the innovator in everyone.

We say YES to CHALLENGES

We value challenges because they produce innovations. We commit to approaching problems with enthusiasm and optimism.

We say YES to TECHNOLOGY

We celebrate the power of technology to transform lives. We commit to helping people use technology creatively and ethically.

We say YES to FUN

We are passionate about our work and about working together. We can't help but share this joyfulness with everyone.

We say YES to INTEGRITY

We value the trust and respect of our community and coworkers. We commit to becoming a place where we do what's right because we love what's right.

Philadelphia Museum of Art, Philadelphia, Pennsylvania

Core Values

The responsible stewardship of the resources that have been entrusted to our care

A dedication to building new and more diverse audiences while deepening their engagement with the visual arts

An unwavering commitment to integrity and excellence

Steadfast belief in the power of the arts to educate, enlighten, and inspire both individuals and society as a whole

Columbus Museum, Columbus, Georgia
  Values: Core beliefs that guide our conduct
    Quality. We believe that the Chattahoochee Valley deserves only the best; we aim to excel at everything we do.
    Accessibility. We exemplify southern hospitality; we are welcoming and friendly to all.
    Collaboration. Partners are essential; we work to build relationships and co-create with organizations and individuals.
    Curiosity. We never stop learning or thinking; we continually push boundaries and explore new territory.
    Stewardship. The Museum will serve in perpetuity; to ensure this, we build and care for our collections, make smart use of our financial resources, and continually invest in our future.
    Accountability. We exist to benefit the community; we demonstrate our success and value.

National WWII Museum, New Orleans, Louisiana
  Commitment to the defense of freedom
  Courage
  Optimism
  Determination
  Sacrifice
  Teamwork
  Generosity
  Volunteerism

About the Museum Trustee Association and the Authors

The Museum Trustee Association was formed as a committee of the American Association of Museums (now known as the American Alliance of Museums) in 1971. Time revealed that the differences of focus, responsibility, and interest between museum professionals and volunteer boards of trustees would be better served by a separate nonprofit organization. The Museum Trustee Association became a separate entity in 1986 and received its federal IRS 501(c)(3) status in 1991. Since then, MTA has been governed by an elected board of directors representing diverse regions of the United States, the Caribbean, Canada, and Mexico, a variety of museum disciplines and sizes, and wide-ranging areas of expertise in trusteeship. All are current or former museum trustees, and several are founders of MTA.

Daryl Fischer founded Musynergy Consulting in 1993 to provide strategic and interpretive planning, audience evaluation, and board development services to museums and other cultural nonprofits. In 2001 she coauthored the first edition of *Building Museum Boards*, followed by *The Leadership Partnership* (2002), *Executive Transitions* (2003), and *Strategic Thinking and Planning* (2004). Her service on numerous nonprofit boards including the Urban Institute for Contemporary Arts (Grand Rapids, Michigan), the Visitor Studies Association, and the Progressive Women's Alliance of the Lakeshore has given her a profound appreciation for the passion, energy, and expertise that board members bring to the organizations they serve. Her consulting practice has taught her that there is no one-size-fits-all formula for maximizing board effectiveness; however, authentic collaboration with staff and community members leads to a whole that is greater than the sum of the parts. Daryl has an MA from the University of Denver and a BA from Colorado College.

Laura B. Roberts is principal of Roberts Consulting, working with cultural nonprofit organizations on strategic planning, assessment, and organizational development. Laura was executive director of the New England Museum Association and the Boston Center for Adult Education. Previously, she was director of education at three history museums. She is the chair of the Central Square Theater in Cambridge, Massachusetts, and formerly chaired the boards of Tufts University Art Gallery, MassHumanities, and First Night Boston. She teaches museum and nonprofit management at Harvard University Extension, Bank Street College of Education, and Northeastern University. Laura holds an MBA from Boston University Questrom School of Business, an MA from the Cooperstown Graduate Program, and a BA from Harvard University.